CONCERNING SPIRITUALS

Volume 2

Authority

House

Submission

CONCERNING SPIRITUALS

<u>VOLUME 2</u>

AUTHORITY

HOUSE

SUBMISSION

Stephen Kaung

Christian Fellowship Publishers, Inc.
New York
Copyright © 2025

Christian Fellowship Publishers, Inc.
New York
All Rights Reserved.

Paperback ISBN: 978-1-68062-185-3
eBook ISBN: 978-1-68062-186-0

Available from the Publishers at:
11515 Allecingie Parkway
Richmond, Virginia 23235
www.c-f-p.com

Printed in the United States of America

Preface

Beginning in 1988, God's servant Stephen Kaung, began ministering God's word at the Northeast Christian Weekend Conference [NCWC]. After sharing on *Heavenly Vision* that first year, he then faithfully shared on matters concerning spiritual realities, year by year for over twenty years at NCWC. (The first three years of ministry [1988-1991] are published under the title *Concerning Spirituals,* Volume 1).

In 1992, our dear brother shared on the very important matter of *Spiritual Authority.* During those sessions he said: "He [God] is working to re-cover His kingdom on this earth ... Our Lord Jesus came into this world to re-establish God's authority." As the church of God, do we know that it is through the obedience of the church to the authority of God, that He is to recover the whole earth"?

The theme of the ministry in 1993 was *Spiritual House.* God has a purpose which He purposed in His beloved Son. And what He has purposed in His Son is a spiritual house, a dwelling place, a home for God in the spirit. Using God's word, brother Kaung addressed such questions as: What is the meaning of God's spiritual house? What characterizes God's house and how is it built?

The third section of this volume contains the ministry on *Spiritual Submission* given during two ministry times in 1994, entitled: What is Spiritual Submission? and How Can We Submit? As our brother concluded these messages, he said: "I do hope there will be a change of atmosphere in the church. I have to weep when I see how God's people fight for power, for authority, and for position. That is not what the church is. Where can you see the spirit of submission? Where can you see that readiness to obey in the church? Where can you see Christ? My prayer is there will be a change of spirit among God's people, that we will see more of the spirit of submission and the actions of obedience."

Contents

Note

The messages contained in this book were spoken by Stephen Kaung during three consecutive Northeast Christian Weekend Conferences (NCWC). These conferences were held during October 1991, 1992, and 1993 at Long Beach Island, New Jersey.

Unless otherwise indicated,
Scripture quotations are from the
New Translation by J. N. Darby.

Part One:
Spiritual Authority

A Look At Spiritual Authority

Romans 13:1—Let every soul be subject to the authorities that are above him. For there is no authority except from God; and those that exist are set up by God.

II Corinthians 10:8—For and if I should boast even somewhat more abundantly of our authority, which the Lord has given to us for building up and not for your overthrowing.

II Corinthians 13:10—On this account I write these things being absent, that being present I may not use severity according to the authority which the Lord has given me for building up, and not for overthrowing.

I Samuel 15:22-23a—And Samuel said, Has Jehovah delight in burnt offerings and sacrifices, as in hearkening to the voice of Jehovah? Behold, obedience is better than sacrifice, attention than the fat of rams. For rebellion is as the sin of divination, and self-will is as iniquity and idolatry.

Philippians 2:5-11—For let this mind be in you which was also in Christ Jesus; who, subsisting in the form of God, did not esteem it an object of rapine to be on an equality with God; but emptied himself, taking a bondman's form, taking his place in the likeness of men; and having been found in figure as a man, humbled himself, becoming obedient even unto death, and that the death of the cross. Wherefore also God highly exalted him, and granted him a name, that which is above every name, that at the name of Jesus every knee should bow, of heavenly and earthly and infernal beings, and every tongue confess that Jesus Christ is Lord to God the Father's glory.

The burden that we have for this time is on the matter of spiritual authority. First of all, I would like to say, do not be afraid of authority. Do not have a kind of unconscious resistance in your mind and in your heart when this word authority is mentioned. Much of this is caused by our misunderstanding of what authority really is. If by the grace of God, we see what authority really is, it is the most blessed thing, and we will welcome it instead of being afraid of it.

At the very outset, we would like to lay down a fundamental truth concerning authority: there is no authority except from God. When the apostle Paul wrote that letter to the Romans, the "authorities" that he mentioned in chapter 13 are delegated authorities. In other words, they are earthly authorities that God has set up. Nevertheless, it does tell us a very fundamental truth that there is no authority except from God. To put it in another way, it simply tells us that God is the only authority in the universe. There is no authority whatsoever except God Himself and what God has given. Now, I do believe that in a way we all know this, but unfortunately, I am afraid that this concept does not really sink into our hearts. It is because of this that there is so much misunderstanding about authority. We mistake something that commonly is accepted as authority without knowing what authority really is. So I do hope that this fundamental truth will really enter into our hearts: there is no authority but God. God is the one and only authority in the universe. Any professed authority that is not from God, that is not God Himself, is not real authority because God is the only authority in the whole universe.

Why is He the authority of the universe? It is because He is God; He is the Creator of all things. All things came from Him and for this reason, He has the right over all things.

This word "authority" in Greek is *exousia*. It comes from an impersonal verb *existi* which means "it is lawful." From the meaning of "the liberty of doing things according to one's pleasure," it has become this word authority, that is, "the authority to exercise power." Authority really means freedom of action, free to act as one wishes. That is what authority really means. God's authority is absolute and unlimited. Because of this we have to give to God absolute obedience and absolute submission.

God is the only authority in the universe. His authority is direct, not delegated. He is the authority because of what He is; His authority is inherent in Him. He *is* the authority. Now it is true, He does delegate authority to others—sometimes to angelic beings, other times to human beings. But even

13

though He delegates authority to others, He has never given up His authority. Furthermore, what He has given is limited; it is not absolute. In other words, He still retains in Himself the authority of the universe. His authority must be obeyed. It cannot be challenged. And if His authority is challenged, there will be consequences that follow. This is the authority of God.

The Nature of God's Authority

Knowing that God is the authority and nobody else, we would like to know the nature of God's authority. I think much of the misunderstanding about authority is because we do not know the nature of authority. That is the reason we cannot distinguish between true authority and false authority. I think it is very, very important for us to know the nature of God's authority.

Authority is Spiritual

First of all, authority is the extension of God Himself. In other words, authority is something that comes out of Him; it is natural with Him. It is the result of who He is, of what He is. It is the expression or the manifestation of His very character; it is part of Him. And because of this, what is the nature of God's authority?

Now, we know that God is Spirit. In John chapter 4, when the Samaritan woman was talking with our Lord Jesus, He gradually led her to the matter of worship. In explaining worship to her, the Lord said, "God is Spirit and He who worships God must worship Him in spirit and truth" (see v. 24). So essentially, God is Spirit. Now if God is Spirit, then the authority that comes out of Him must be spiritual in nature. So, authority is spiritual. It is not something that you put on. It is something that comes out of what He is. It is spiritual; it is not positional.

It is true that God does have a position. We sing that song, "We Place You on the Highest Place." He has the highest position; that is true. But His position is because of what He is, not because of what it is made to Him. His position is the result of His spirituality. Because He is Spirit, therefore His authority is spiritual in nature. It is not something to be grasped at, but His authority is inherent in Himself. In Philippians, it is said of our Lord Jesus, that He, the Son of God, is equal with God. That is His position; but that is not something to be grasped at because it is His.

One day our Lord Jesus was on His last trip to Jerusalem before His crucifixion. As He was approaching Jerusalem, His disciples thought this was the time of the glorification of their Master. They thought this was the time that the Lord Jesus would claim His kingdom. It *is* true this was the time of His glorification, but His glorification was not assuming the throne on earth. On the contrary, if you read the Scripture, you find that the glorification He was talking about actually was His crucifixion, but the disciples did not understand that. They thought the Lord was going to Jerusalem to receive His kingdom. So that was a very crucial time for them.

During the three and a half years the disciples followed the Lord Jesus, they were arguing among themselves all the time about which of them was the greatest. Again and again the Lord tried to correct them and instruct them, but somehow it did not sink into their hearts. So even at the last minute, they were still thinking of this same thing, and now it was the last opportunity.

Do you remember that story in Matthew chapter 20? John and James got their mother, who was, humanly speaking, an aunt to our Lord Jesus, to plead for them. They came to the Lord Jesus and said, "Lord, give us what we ask for." And the Lord said, "What do you want?" The mother said, "... that these my two sons may sit, one on Thy right hand and one on Thy left in Thy kingdom" (v. 21). This is position, and they thought that authority was a matter of position. If they can get that position on the right and on the left, then they could have all the authority of the right and of the left.

How did our Lord Jesus respond to them? He said, "Are you able to drink the cup that I am going to drink? Are you able to be baptized with the baptism that I am going to be baptized with?"

Actually, John and James did not understand what the Lord was talking about because their mind was full of this matter of the right and the left hand. Without even considering what the Lord said, without even knowing what the Lord really meant, because they wanted that position so much, they said, "Yes. We will be baptized with the baptism that you are baptized with, although we do not even know what that baptism means. We will drink the cup that you are going to drink, even though we do not know what that cup is. But we want that position."

And the Lord said, "It is not for Me to give. It is for the Father to decide." In other words, here the Lord was saying, "You must drink the cup that I am going to drink."

Now of course, you quickly connect this *cup* with the scene of Gethsemane where our Lord, on the night of His betrayal, entered into that garden. He was deeply depressed, and He asked three of His disciples to wait there and watch with Him. He went forward a stone's throw, and there He agonized in prayer: "Father, if it is possible, let this cup be passed from Me. But not My will, Thy will be done." That is the cup that He was talking about (see Matthew 26:36-39).

What is the cup? The cup is a portion. Even though the cup that our Lord Jesus was talking about was a bitter cup, it represents the will of God. Whatever the will of God may be, whether it is bitter or sweet, "Thy will be done."

When our Lord Jesus, who was equal with God, emptied Himself, He took the form of a bondslave, even the fashion of a man. In doing that, He laid down all the glory, the power, and the honor that was rightfully His as God. He laid everything down. He did not lay down His deity. No, He could not do that. He is still God. But He laid down everything that belonged to God—power, glory, honor, majesty, worship—He laid down all these things. He emptied Himself of all these things in order to become a man. In order to become a bondslave before God, the Lord gave up a great deal. But even though He gave up all the glory and honor and power in connection with His deity when He came to be a man, these did not touch His character. He is still holy, He is still perfect, He is still pure. These do not touch His very being, His character.

However, in the garden of Gethsemane, why did our Lord agonize so much over this matter of the cup? It is because in drinking that cup, it touched His very being. It touched His very character—He who knew no sin was to be made sin for us—that is the reason He shrank back as a perfect man. But even so, because of the love that He had for us, He was willing to be defiled, contaminated, completely misunderstood, rejected by God and men, in order to save us. Think of the love of Christ! That is the cup He was talking about, and He was willing to drink that cup to the fullest.

The Lord said, "Are you able to drink the cup that I am going to drink?" In other words, are you willing to accept the Father's will, whatever it may be? You know what we are: if it is a sweet cup we enjoy it; if it is a bitter cup we want it to be passed from us. But the Lord said, "If you really want authority, it is not a matter of position, it is a matter of spirituality."

What is spirituality? It simply means that here is a person who is willing to accept the will of God, whatever it may be. "Are you able to be baptized with the baptism that I am baptized with?" Of course, the baptism that He refers to is the cross. At the beginning of His ministry, He was baptized by John the Baptist in order to fulfill all righteousness (see Matthew 3:15). That baptism is really a type of the cross where He was going to be crucified.

What is baptism? Baptism simply means death. You do not baptize a person who is living because you will bury him alive. We see that we have died in Christ Jesus, we have died to our old man; therefore, we go into the water to be baptized—to be buried out of sight. Then as we come out of the water, we are a new creation, a new person. That is what baptism means, and that is what the cross means. The cross is the place where Christ was crucified. The cross is the place where you and I were crucified. The cross is the place where self is denied and is laid down. That is the baptism.

So the Lord said, "Are you able to be baptized with the baptism that I am baptized with?" In other words, are you able to deny yourself? Are you able to take up your cross and follow Him to the very end that you will be crucified? Are you willing for "self" to be completely crucified? Are you *willing* to do that? Are you *able* to do that? It is not a matter of position; it is a matter of denying yourself and laying down your life. It is a spiritual matter. Maybe we are willing, but are we able?

Dear brothers and sisters, first of all we will see that authority is spiritual in nature. If you really desire authority, then remember it is not just something for the asking. And if you ask for authority, do you know what you are asking for? You are asking for the cup; you are asking for the baptism. And only those who, by the grace of God, are not only willing, but are able to drink the cup and be baptized with the baptism, then the Father will decide where they will be seated.

So, I am afraid this whole matter of authority is completely misunderstood; but if we can really understand the nature of authority, then I do believe it will save us lots of trouble and problems. You may not even dare ask for authority, although it is something to ask for, but not for yourself. Later on you will find that authority is a most glorious thing. Anyway, the first nature of authority is spiritual, not positional.

Authority is of Life

Secondly, authority is of life. "With thee is the fountain of life. In thy light shall we see light" (Psalm 36:9). God is authority because He is the fountain of life. He is life itself, and life always carries authority. The apostle John says:

> That which was from the beginning, that which we have heard, which we have seen with our eyes, that which we have contemplated, and our hands handled, concerning the word of life; (and the life has been manifested …) that which we have seen and heard we report to you, that you may have fellowship with us; and our fellowship is indeed with the Father and His Son Jesus Christ. And these things write we unto you that your joy may be full (I John 1:1-4).

In the Gospel of John it says, "In Him was life, and the life was the light of men" (1:4). In other words, you find that our God is the God of life. He is full of life. And He is not only full of life, but He gives life. Everything comes out of His life and that is why He is the authority over all. Authority is not something you assume; authority is the result of life.

I do not have a good illustration, but I will use this as an imperfect illustration. Why is it that in our families the children must obey the parents? One reason is that they have lived longer than we have, and they have more experience of life. Or we

21

may put it in another way: they gave us life. Of course, God gave us life, but our parents do give us life; they nourish us, and they bring us up. The parents have that position as parents, not because they assumed that position, but because they have more life experience. That is why they have more authority over the children.

In the church of God, when you consider this matter of authority, you find the Bible tells us of the elders. Are those elders older physically in age or are they older spiritually? I think the latter probably is more correct, but of course the growth of spiritual life takes time too. In other words, in the church you have the elders, and the elders represent the government of God. It is not because some people assume this position. It is because among the brothers and sisters they seem to have more of the life of Christ in them. They seem to have more manifestation of spiritual life. And because their life is at least a step ahead of us, therefore they represent more of the authority of God. So, it is not something that anybody can assume. It is because of the life of Christ within them. In fact, the more spiritual life you have, the more authority there is.

For instance, we are all familiar with Barnabas and Paul. In Acts chapter 13, the five prophets and teachers were ministering to the Lord, and the Holy Spirit said, "Set me apart Barnabas and Saul for the work I am going to send them to." And these two men were set apart as apostles. They went forth, and the young man John Mark was with them as an attendant. So they traveled from Antioch and on to Cyprus.

As you read the Bible, you find that when they went forward, it was always Barnabas and Saul. In other words, even with the two apostles and with the young man John Mark, there was a divine order, but that divine order was not something that was arranged or assumed. Barnabas did not assume that because he knew the Lord before Saul, therefore he would take the lead and Saul would just follow him; or because He was the one who introduced Saul to the saints in Jerusalem, then he had to be the leader, as if to say, "Everybody was afraid of you, but I believed in you, and I introduced you to Peter." Nor did he assume that because he found Saul in Tarsus and brought him to Antioch where he was under his apprenticeship for a whole year, that he would take the lead and Saul would just follow. No, there was nothing arranged; there was nothing assumed. The Holy Spirit said, "Set me apart Barnabas and Saul." Somehow there was an order there—not assumed, but of life.

But strangely, you find when they traveled to Cyprus, on the way, suddenly, the order began to change. The Holy Spirit, in the word of God, tells us it is "Paul and his company" (see Acts 13:13). Saul changed his name to Paul, and Paul means little—the *little* and his company. Now, John Mark was not happy about it because he was a relative of Barnabas. When he discovered that the order had changed, he could not accept it, so he left. But thank God, Barnabas knew the Lord, and without any protest, willingly he took the second position. It is not a matter of trying to get to a position; it is a manifestation of life. Somehow, the Christ-life in Paul seemed to be more manifested than the Christ-life in Barnabas, and because of that, Paul took the lead.

It is a matter of life. Now if we can see this, then there should be no argument. You cannot argue about life. If life is there, it is there. If life is not there, no matter how you argue, it is not there. If there is more measure of Christ in that brother, it is there; and if you do not have that measure of Christ, it is evident; everybody knows it. It is something that you cannot argue. You cannot assume it because it is purely a matter of life. When a person begins to argue over this matter of authority, you know for sure that he is outside of life.

Furthermore, since authority is of life, when a person is in life with the Lord, there is authority, but the moment he is not living in the life of Christ, that authority is gone. This is very important, and I will explain it later on. So authority is of life and not something anybody can assume.

Authority is in Giving

Thirdly, authority is in giving, not in gaining. Think of God. Our God is the great Giver. He is so rich; He is so full. The fullness of the Godhead is something beyond our comprehension. We cannot understand and yet we find all the time God is giving, giving, giving. God so loved the world that He gave His only begotten Son. Christ so loved the church and gave Himself for it. But our whole concept of authority is in gaining. "If I have authority, I gain a lot for myself. Then I can force people to do what I want them to do, and I can gain a lot." No, authority is in giving, not in gaining.

There is authority in giving. The one who gives has authority over the one who receives. That is very natural. The more you give, the more authority you have. Our Lord Jesus said, "I give Myself a ransom for many." Because He gave Himself as a ransom for many, therefore the many come under His authority.

Authority is in Serving

Fourthly, in connection with this, authority is in serving. You know that famous verse in the Gospel of Mark where our Lord Jesus said, "I do not come to be served, but to serve and to give My life a ransom for many" (see 10:45).

The disciples were arguing among themselves over who was the greater one. So our Lord began to teach them a lesson. He said, "In this world, those who rule, lord over other people. Those who are great, exercise authority; but it is not so among you. Among you, the great is to be your servant, the first is to be your bondslave. For I do not come to be ministered to, but to minister, and to give my life a ransom for many" (see Mark 10:42-45).

Brothers and sisters, we all want to be great. We all want to be first. In the world, the great and the first are those who sit high up and rule over other people. That is the way in the world; and the world's concept of authority is a position. When you get to that position, then you can lord over all those other people. Then you are great. You become first among them. But the Lord said, "But it is not so among you."

I am afraid, brothers and sisters, we have not heard the Lord. When the Lord said, "It is not so among you," in our mind, we say, "It is still so." If you understand what the Lord is talking about, it is very revolutionary. The Lord said that the whole concept of world authority has to be thrown out of the window. Do not ever let any of that concept contaminate you. Not so, not so in your midst. This is the world.

What is authority in your midst? What does it mean to be great? To be first? The Lord said, "The great among you is to be servant of all." Now, to be great and to be the servant of the Lord sounds good. But the Lord said, "To be great among you is to be the servant of all." That is difficult. Do you want to be great? You have to be servant to all of your brothers and sisters.

Who are your masters? Of course, the Lord is your Master, but aside from the Lord, our brothers and sisters are our masters. We think that if we are great, we become master of our brothers and sisters. They are our servants; we give orders and tell them what they should do. But no, the Lord said, "That is the world's concept of authority. My concept of authority is that if you want to be great, serve your brothers and sisters. Serve them as if they were your masters." Now, are you willing to be great?

More than that the Lord said, "If you want to be first, (not only great, but first) you become a bondslave of all." A servant can still have their say and if they are not willing, they can quit. But a bondslave has no right whatsoever. If they want to be the first among their brothers and sisters, then they have to be a bondslave, not only to Christ, but to the brothers and sisters.

Are we willing to be slaves to our brothers and sisters? That is what it is. That is where authority lies. It is in serving. The Lord said, "I did not come to be served, but to serve." Who serves most? Our Lord Jesus. He served us to the extent of not only washing our feet, but He served us to the extent that He gave up His life as a ransom for all. That is how He serves us and that is why He is great and why He is the First. That is why He has authority over us. The one who serves has authority over those whom He serves. That is the nature of authority.

Authority is in Love

Fifthly, authority is in love. We often think that love and authority are incompatible. If there is love, we think there should be no authority exercised. In other words, if we really love, we will let people do anything they like. Whether it is right or wrong, whether it pleases us or not, because we love, love, love, therefore we love and there is no discipline, no authority, no order—nothing. On the other hand, we think that authority is by force—forcing people to do what they do not want to do, demanding that people do what they do not want to do. Now of course, if that is our concept of love and authority, they are incompatible. But God is love and God is authority. Love is His nature; authority is His manifestation, His right. These two things do not contradict each other. These two things go together. I would even dare to say that love *is* authority. Authority is love—sacrificial love—giving up one's self to serve the good of the others. Now if this is authority, isn't it love? If you really love, there must be discipline, and you cannot discipline if there is no authority. So, you find that this matter of love and authority are really joined together. Authority has to be exercised in love and love must chastise. In Hebrews chapter 12, it says that our heavenly Father chastises us because He loves us as His sons. If He does not chastise us, then we are illegitimate children, not sons. Therefore authority and love cannot be divorced;

they are together. That is the very nature of authority.

Brothers and sisters, do we now understand what authority really is? In understanding authority, we understand God. I feel that this is something we have to understand.

The Purpose of Authority

What is the purpose of authority? Why is there authority? We say that God is the Creator of the universe. He created the world by the word of His power. His word not only has power, but it has authority. There is a difference between authority and power. Authority is the right to exercise power and power is the ability to do things. The word of God has not only power, but the word of God has authority. He says it and it is done. He speaks a word, and the thing is done because His word is full of authority and full of power. He not only framed the world by the word of His power, but even this whole world subsists today by His word.

After God created the universe, He used His authority to bring this world into order. Everything God created was put in order under His government, under His authority. So there was no chaos, no disorder; everything was as He desired. Unfortunately, His authority was challenged. When His authority was unchallenged, the universe that He created was in perfect order. Not only the physical universe, but even the spiritual was in perfect order. Not only did all the stars revolve in their orbits as God had ordained, but even the angelic beings ministered unto God as they were assigned. Everything was in perfect order because His authority sustained that order.

Unfortunately, one day, that order and authority was challenged. Lucifer, the archangel, was probably the first created angel. God put him in the highest position, aside from God Himself. He was an anointed cherub. If we may use this metaphor, He was the cherub that stood behind the throne of God, nearest to God. He was given wisdom, skill, dominion, rule, and power. But unfortunately, he got proud of himself; he wanted to be equal with God.

Now who is equal with God? The beloved Son, and that is not something to be grasped at because He *is* God. But for Lucifer to try to be equal with God, he had to grasp something that did not belong to him. And because of his rebellion there was judgment. The world was thrown into disorder: *tohu* and *bohu* ("waste and empty" see Genesis 1:2). Everything was in ruin, in emptiness, purposeless, and covered with darkness. God repaired the earth and brought it back to order. He gave dominion to man to rule over all the things created, but unfortunately, man sinned and threw this world again into disorder, under the curse. We are still living in this cursed world.

Authority is for Building Up

It is because of what has happened in prehistoric times and in historical times that our concept of authority has become negative. In other words, whenever we think of authority we think of overthrowing, overturning, punishment, and judgment. But in the beginning, it was not so.

What is the purpose of authority? The apostle Paul said again and again, "The authority that God has given to me is for building up, not for overthrowing" (see II Corinthians 10:8, 13:10). Do we really understand this? The basic purpose, or the fundamental meaning of authority is to build up. It is very positive, very beautiful, very glorious. It is not for overthrowing. In other words, authority has a two-fold meaning. One is positive, which is primary and original—it is for building up. One is negative and secondary—it is overthrowing. There can be no building up without authority.

What builds up the church? Two things—life and authority, and these two things are one. If there is no authority, there can be no building up because everybody wants to have their own will and their own way. How can you build brothers and sisters together if that is the case? It is like the children of Israel at the time of the judges. At the very end of the book of Judges, chapter 21:25, the Holy Spirit commented on the hundreds of years of history of the children of Israel in Canaan: "There was no king in Israel; every man did what was right in his own eyes." There was no building up because there was no king, no authority to build up. You need authority to join people together and build them up.

Our Lord Jesus said, "I will build My church upon this rock and the gates of hades shall not prevail against it" (see Matthew 16:18). When did He say that? He said that after Peter confessed, "You are the Christ, the Son of the living God." As the Son of the living God, He has authority. As the Christ, the sent One of God, He came to accomplish that work of redemption; and because of His obedience to the Father, He was given authority. He not only had authority as God, but He was given authority as the Son of Man, as Christ. God had made Him Christ and Lord, and because He has authority, therefore He said, "I will build My church."

In Matthew chapter 28 we find the great commission: "Go ye and disciple the nations, baptizing them in the name of the Father, the Son, and the Holy Spirit, and teach them all the things that I have enjoined You. And I will be with you until the end of the age" (see vv. 19-20).

Now, how can the church accomplish this great commission of not only evangelizing the world, but discipling the nations? How can you disciple without discipline? How can you discipline without authority? And where is the authority? In the verse before that the Lord said, "All authority has been given to me in heaven and on earth." The word there is not power; in the original it is *authority*. "All authority has been given to me in heaven and on earth. Go therefore … " (v. 18). It is on that authority that we are able to disciple the nations, teach them all the things that God has enjoined us and prepare the kingdom for the King. It is authority.

So dear brothers and sisters, authority is something to be welcomed because without authority there can be no building up. If the Lord does not have authority over your life, do you think that your spiritual life will be built up? "For where two or three are gathered together unto My name, there am I in the midst of them" (Matthew 18:20). What does it mean? Two or three are gathered together unto His name, the name that is above every name, and to that name, every knee shall bow, and every tongue confess that Jesus is Lord. That is authority. It is authority when we put ourselves under His name, that is, under His authority; then His presence will be there. And it is His presence that builds the church. There is nothing more glorious than when you really see what authority is and what it does. How foolish we are to despise authority, thinking it is useless. Whether it is individual or corporate, there can be no building up without authority. It is authority that builds. Let us welcome it.

But then, of course, there is the other side of it. When authority is rejected, despised, and unaccepted, then you find it is for overthrowing. Nevertheless, even with the overthrowing, it is for the purpose of building up. It is not just overthrowing. Our God is very positive; He is never negative. Even in overthrowing, it is for the purpose of building up. He cannot build when there is opposition, when there is resistance. So this resistance has to be overturned, has to be taken away, taken aside; and in doing that, you find overthrowing. There will be judgment, there will be chastisement, but remember again, this is a by-product. It is secondary, not primary.

If you really see authority, there is nothing to be afraid of, but it is something to look forward to because it builds you up. However, if there is rebellion in your heart, then authority is a terrible thing because God does not allow His authority to be challenged.

Our Response to Authority

What is our response to authority? I think if we really know what the nature of authority is and what authority does, then it is quite natural for us to see that our response to authority is nothing less than obedience. Obedience is the natural response to authority. There is nothing that pleases God more than listening to Him: "Obedience is better than sacrifice." Nothing pleases God more than obedience, and obedience is the natural response to authority. Unfortunately, we are willing to give God anything and everything except obedience.

We are willing to give Him sacrifices, lots of them—the fat of rams—but we do not want to listen to Him or obey Him.

But look at our Lord Jesus. What an obedient Son He was! As God, He knew no obedience because you cannot connect obedience with God. He is God. He obeys nobody. We try to make Him obey us, but we cannot do that. He is God, but He learned obedience when He was on earth as a man, the Son of Man. He learned obedience through the things He suffered. Obedience is a hard lesson even with our Lord when He was on earth because He had a perfect soul. In other words, there was no sin in Him; there was no rebellion in Him, but He was a man. He had His will—a perfect will, a sinless will—and yet even He had to learn obedience through the things which He suffered. How He denied Himself! So our Lord is a perfect example. But He is not only an example. In Hebrews it says that He learned obedience through the things which He suffered, and because He has learned the lesson, He has become the Originator of our eternal salvation. In other words, He is not only the example of obedience, He also gives us the life of obedience.

God is the perfect authority; therefore, to Him we render absolute obedience and absolute submission. Obedience is an act; submission is an attitude. We need to give to God the attitude of absolute submission—no quarreling with Him. We need to give Him absolute obedience—no rebellion against Him. But of course, when God puts man over us to represent His authority, then we should give them absolute submission, as long as we are under, but not absolute obedience. We are to obey God rather than obey man. If any person misrepresents God's authority and it so happens that God puts you under his authority, then you can render absolute submission, but you do not need to give absolute obedience because you have to obey God.

The way to authority is through obedience. Our Lord Jesus emptied Himself and became obedient even unto death, and that the death of the cross. Therefore, God has highly exalted Him and given Him a name that is above every name. So in other words, the way to authority is through obedience.

Signs of Those Who Know Authority

Finally, what are the indispensable signs of those who know authority? If you have read *Spiritual Authority* by our dear brother, Watchman Nee, you find he mentions a few things. Dear brothers and sisters, authority is something that we need to recognize, we need to know. Not knowing authority is a great defect in our spiritual life; and it is not only a defect, it is an obstacle, a hindrance. So we need to know authority, recognize authority, and there are five indispensable signs.

Number One—Wherever you go, try to find authority to submit to. If you go anywhere and all you are looking for is: "Who will submit to me?" you do not know what authority is. But if you really know what authority is, wherever you go, when you are with your brothers and sisters, you are looking for authority, God's authority, that you can submit to because it is the most pleasant thing to do. Now that is a sure sign that you know authority.

Number Two—If you really know authority, you will be tender and soft. People who do not know authority are hard people.

Number Three—People who know authority never want to be authority. How much more blessed to submit to authority than to be authority because the responsibility is too great. So, you never want to be in authority. That shows you know what authority is.

Number Four—If you really know what authority is, you will not talk too much. Somehow, authority shuts your mouth up. If you really know what authority is, lots of murmuring stops, lots of talking stops. It is very true.

Number Five—The last sign of people who know authority is that they are sensitive to every lawlessness. So may the Lord help us.

Dear heavenly Father, we do feel that
we are standing on holy ground because
Thou art THE authority of the universe

and we are under Thy authority. Lord, we do pray that by Thy grace we may be a people who know Thy authority, not only to submit and to obey, but even by Thy mercy to represent Thy authority. Lord, we do acknowledge that we are disqualified, whether in obedience or in authority. Only Thy grace, Thy mercy can make us so. We just again humble ourselves before Thee. We want to tremble at Thy word and let Thy word really touch our hearts that we may repent and return to Thy original thought on authority. Make it a reality among Thy people. We ask in Thy precious name. Amen.

Delegated Authority

Romans 13:1-5—Let every soul be subject to the authorities that are above him. For there is no authority except from God; and those that exist are set up by God. So that he that sets himself in opposition to the authority resists the ordinance of God; and they who thus resist shall bring sentence of guilt on themselves. For rulers are not a terror to a good work, but to an evil one. Dost thou desire then not to be afraid of the authority? practice what is good, and thou shall have praise from it; for it is God's minister to thee for good. But if thou practicest evil, fear; for it bears not the sword in vain; for it is God's minister, an avenger of wrath to him that does evil. Wherefore it is necessary to be subject, not only on account of wrath, but also on account of conscience.

Matthew 8:9—For I also am a man under authority, having under me soldiers, and I say to this one, Go, and he goes; and to another, Come, and he comes; and to my bondman, Do this, and he does it.

John 5:19-20, 26-27, 30—Jesus therefore answered and said to them, Verily, verily, I say to you, The Son can do nothing of himself save whatever He sees the Father doing: for whatever things he does, these things also the Son does in like manner. For the Father loves the Son and shews him all things which he himself does; and he will shew him greater works than these, that ye may wonder. For even as the Father has life in himself, so he has given to the Son also to have life in himself, and has given him authority to ex- ecute judgment also, because he is Son of man. I cannot do anything of myself; as I hear, I judge, and my judgment is righteous, because I do not seek my will, but the will of him that has sent me.

John 8:28-29—Jesus therefore said to them, When ye shall have lifted up the Son of man, then ye shall know that I am [he], and that I do nothing of myself, but as the Father has taught me I speak these things. And he that has sent me is with me; he has not left me alone, because I do always the things that are pleasing to him.

Ephesians 5:21—Submitting yourselves to one another in the fear of Christ.

There is a fundamental truth that we must al- ways remember: there is no authority except from God. Or to put it in another way, in this universe, in the creation, God is the one and only authority; whatever is not God, or is not of God, is a counter- feit. Only that which is God Himself, only that which is given by God, is true authority. How dif- ferent God's authority, true authority, is from the authority that we usually understand and accept because authority is God's right. It is something that comes out of Himself; therefore His authority carries His very character in it. God's authority is spiritual; it is not positional. God's authority is life; it is not something that you assume. God's authority is giving, not getting. God's authority is serving, not being served. And God's authority is love. These are the nature of authority.

The purpose of authority is not for overthrowing, even though this is our impression. It is because we are a rebellious people. God's authority is primarily for building up. It is through God's authority that there can be any building up of our spiritual life. It takes God's authority to do that. If you reject God's authority in your life, you will never be built up. If you are saved, you will remain a babe in Christ. It is the authority of God that builds up the church, otherwise the church would never be built. How precious is God's authority. It is not something to be rejected, but it is something we should look forward to and welcome. Our response to authority is to obey.

Now we would like to continue on with a further look into authority—delegated authority. Dear brothers and sisters, we say God is authority, and I do not believe that anyone here will challenge this statement. Probably, we think that it is easy for us to obey God as authority. In other words, we have no problem with God as authority. If you have any problem with that, you are in very serious trouble. We have no trouble accepting that God is the authority. We have no trouble, at least mentally, in accepting that we should obey God's direct authority because, after all, He is God, and we are His created beings. However, although we accept it mentally, when we come to our actual living, how often we challenge God's authority.

For instance, take the apostle Peter. We find that in his life, more than once, he challenged God's authority. On that night of the betrayal of our Lord Jesus, the Lord knew that He came from the Father; He knew that He was going back to His Father; He knew that He was their Lord and their Master, but He loved them, and He loved them to the uttermost. And on that night, He washed His disciple's feet to show His love to them. He is the authority, and that authority is expressed in love, in loving and humble service. But when He came to Peter, Peter said: "Lord, what are you doing here? Do You wash my feet? (see John 13:6).

Now, who is Lord, the Lord Jesus or Peter? Did Peter really learn the lesson that evening? Hardly. Even after our Lord died, resurrected, ascended, and the Holy Spirit came, and Peter was greatly used by God, one day, he was on the rooftop praying in Joppa. He was a little bit hungry because it was noon time, and people were cooking food there. So while he was on the rooftop praying (probably thinking of eating), God used that opportunity to give him a vision. In that vision he saw a great white sheet coming down from heaven right before him, and he looked into it and saw all those unclean animals, and creeping things, and fowls. And the voice said, "Rise, Peter, kill, and eat."

How strong was Peter's tradition! Tradition has a very strong hold on a person. Even though Peter was hungry, tradition was so strong, he said, "Lord, not so. This cannot be done because I have never eaten anything unclean."

And the voice said, "What God has cleansed, let no man say is unclean." It happened three times and the white sheet went up into heaven, so that Peter wondered what the vision might mean (see Acts 10:9-16).

Do we laugh at Peter? Let us laugh at ourselves. How often we say, "Lord, Lord, not so." Even though, mentally, we do accept the direct authority of God, we think we have no problem with that, but we still have a problem. How we need to see Him as God, that He has absolute authority over us! And to His authority, there should be no questioning, no argument, but immediate, absolute submission and absolute obedience.

Now we would like to share on this matter of delegated authority, and this is where all the problems are. God *is* authority. He uses His authority to create all things, to maintain all things, and to govern all things that the whole universe will be in harmony and in order. If God should keep His authority all to Himself, how simple it would be, but it is His good pleasure to delegate authority. God is God. That is His right, and if He wants to delegate authority that is what He can do. No one can question Him. It seems that this is God's pleasure. Now maybe there is a reason behind it. Of course, today, we seem to catch a little bit of what the reason is, but still it is beyond our understanding.

The Beginning of Rebellion

Why should God delegate authority and not just keep authority to Himself—everything direct and nothing else? How simple it would be. There would not be all these problems. But it pleases God to delegate authority. Even in the first world, He delegated His authority to angelic beings. You remember in the Scripture it tells us there are angels and archangels, there are seraphim and cherubim, there are principalities and authorities. In other words, after God created the universe, He delegated His authority to angelic beings, some with greater authority, some with lesser authority. All these delegated authorities are God's servants.

Angels are God's servants. They serve God under God's authority. And under God's authority, with the authority that God had given to them, they governed this universe for the glory of God. Everything was beautiful; everything expressed the glory of God. Everything served the purpose of God. All these angelic beings were under the authority of God when they exercised the authority given to them. We say again that authority is not something assumed; authority is something given. These angelic beings were given authority, and as long as they exercised the authority given by God, under God, everything worked perfectly.

In that prehistoric time, one archangel—beautiful, talented, highly positioned, gifted—was given great authority and dominion by God. Unfortunately, somehow an evil thought entered into his mind; in other words, he began to be conscious of himself. In the beginning, nothing, no one, was conscious of himself. The only consciousness in this universe was God. All these angelic beings were only conscious of God. They were not conscious of themselves, they were not conscious of their positions, they were not conscious of their gifts. They were only conscious of the God whom they served. Everything was received from God, and everything returned to God. The beginning of rebellion is *self*-consciousness.

One archangel began to be conscious of himself. He began to be conscious of his beauty, of his power, of his position, of his skills, of the authority that had been given to him. Before he began to be conscious of himself, he wanted to use all the authorities and powers and gifts and beauty that God had given him to serve God. Now, instead, he wanted to use all these to serve himself, and to do that a rebellious spirit came upon him. Instead of being under the authority of God, he wanted to set up his own authority. Instead of serving God's kingdom, he wanted to establish his own kingdom, his own dominion. For this reason, he was cast out. He turned himself into Satan, the adversary of God. Evidently, our solar system at that time was under his control. Oh, how he affected not only the earth that was under his control, but he affected even other angels. He was able to instill that poison, that rebellious spirit into one-third of the angelic hosts and to lead them into rebellion. And he was able to turn this earth that God has created into ruin and darkness.

All these things happened because, when God's authority was challenged, God would not allow it. His discipline and judgment came. That is true. But in another sense, it was the result of that rebellious spirit. Wherever there is a rebellious spirit, it brings in darkness, it brings in ruin, it brings in emptiness, that is, purposelessness. This archangel Lucifer became self-conscious and wanted to make himself equal with God, an authority in himself, instead of being under authority and functioning with the authority God had given him. He was cast out and his dominion turned into ruin and darkness.

But God did not give up. He did not give up the idea of delegated authority. If it were you or me, after such a thing took place, we would say, "It is better not to delegate authority. I will just hold it all by myself." But no, God is different from us. Even though Satan seemed to set up his own kingdom, the kingdom of darkness, even though Satan rebelled against God's authority, and he was under God's judgment, yet we know one thing: he was still under God's authority. He tried to pull himself out from God's authority and set up his own authority, but he was still under God's authority. Satan could not do anything he wanted to do. Even when he tries to tempt us, he has to get permission from God; he is still under God's authority.

So, no matter how you want to free yourself from God's authority, you just cannot get out because He is *the* authority of the universe. There is no way out. You only bring judgment upon yourself, trouble upon yourself. Thank God, He did not give up the idea of delegating authority. There must be a reason behind it, a very glorious reason behind it.

The Creation of Man

We do not know how long it lasted, but we know from the word of God that the Spirit of God hovered upon the face of the deep, like a hen brooding over an egg. He used His warmth, His love to repair this ruined earth. And on the sixth day, God did a most marvelous thing. It was something He had never done even in the first creation. He decided to create mankind in His own image after His likeness. God had never done that. He created beautiful, glorious angelic beings, but He did not create them in His own image. Now, even after the catastrophe that happened to Him, He did not go backward; He took a step forward. He created man lower than the angels, and yet He created man in His own image. In other words, when He created man, God gave him the capacity to receive

His life into them. He knew that the only safe way to safeguard delegated authority is His own life. So He created man with a capacity to receive His own life. Then, He gave dominion to man over the fowls of the air, over the animals of the field, and over the fishes of the sea. And God put the tree of life in the middle of the garden. In other words, God was saying, "I still delegate My authority. But remember, the secret of being My delegated authority is to receive My life. That is the safeguard."

The Fall of Man

Now again, man sinned. Instead of receiving the life of God into them (so that when they exercised the authority God had given them, they would be safe and secure under His life), they ate the tree of the knowledge of good and evil. In other words, they developed their self-consciousness. They wanted to make themselves God in everything. When that happened, curse came upon this earth. The ground began to grow thistles and thorns. Do you know what thorns are? Thorns are aborted fruits. God's purpose is to bear fruit, but instead of bearing fruit, it was aborted. It did not arrive at its end; it became thorns. That is the curse. Whenever God's authority is rejected, there will be curse; and the greatest curse is that you never arrive at God's end.

God Sets up Authorities

We would say that since God had tried twice, surely that should teach Him a lesson. But God did not learn that lesson. Thank God for that! God still did not give up. His desire of delegating authority is still there. He never changes. In Romans chapter 13, it says that there is no authority except from God and the authorities which exist are set up by God. God still sets up authorities upon this earth. We find that in the nations there are kings, rulers, and government. "And it is He [God] who changes times and seasons, who deposes kings and sets up kings" (see Daniel 2:21). And in that song of Mary in Luke chapter 1, she said, "He has put down rulers from thrones, and exalted the lowly" (v. 52).

In other words, God still delegates authority. In this world, He sets up kings and rulers. These are God's ministers. They are set up by God to serve God's purpose; they are to serve God for good, not for evil. That is the reason why if you do not want to be afraid of authorities, do good. Not only does He set up authorities in the government and in the nations, but He sets up authorities in our homes. Our parents are authorities set up by God. Even in the church, God sets up delegated authorities. God has chosen elders to represent His authority in the church. God still delegates authority. He loves to do that.

What is delegated authority? When the authority of God is delegated, what does it mean? It means that those who are delegated authorities are to represent God. It is a tremendous responsibility! So far as God is concerned, for Him to delegate authority is a great risk. So far as we are concerned, to be delegated authority is a great, serious responsibility because we are to represent God. The sin of misrepresentation is a very serious sin. Moses served God with all faithfulness, but towards the end, his spirit was provoked, and he did something he never should have done. He struck the rock twice and said, "Hear now, you rebels: shall we give you water out of this rock?" (see Numbers 20:10). He misrepresented God's authority; he misused God's authority. He misrepresented God because now the children of Israel could say, "So this is what God is like." But no, God is not like that. For this reason he was not allowed to enter into the Promised Land.

Brothers and sisters, if we know what delegated authority is, we will not so very much desire to be so delegated. Anyone who desires to be God's delegated authority is disqualified from being God's delegated authority. Remember this.

There are two things that we would like to consider before the Lord on this matter of delegated authority: those who are being delegated authority, that is, those who are in authority for God, and those who are under God's delegated authority. When God delegates authority to a person, they to represent God in whatever they do. Whenever that authority is being exercised, it has to express God.

It is not to express themselves, but it is to express God. Whenever they do not express God and expresses themselves, it is a misrepresentation; and this is a serious sin in the sight of God.

A Man with Authority

There is one man who shows us what delegated authority really is and that man is our Lord Jesus. He being God is the very principle of direct authority. He is God. But when our Lord Jesus emptied Himself and became a man on this earth, He is the perfect embodiment of what delegated authority is. When He came to this earth, He has no position whatsoever. Even though He is the son of David, and yet He was not born in Jerusalem. He was not born in a palace. He was born in Bethlehem, a tiny city, in a manger. He had no position on this earth. He had never been to a rabbinical school. He had no status whatsoever. So, if you look at our Lord Jesus, there is nothing outwardly that gave Him authority. Yet, while our Lord Jesus was on earth, He was a man of authority.

We are all familiar with the Sermon on the Mount. And when our Lord Jesus finished delivering that sermon, all those who heard Him said, "He is different from our scribes because He teaches with authority." Even today, when we read Matthew chapters 5, 6, and 7, we will come to the same conclusion: we hear words coming from a man with authority.

The words of our Lord Jesus are full of authority. In Luke chapter 7, the sickness of a centurion's servant was healed with a word. That centurion understood authority. When his servant was sick, he asked the Lord to come and heal him, but he said: "Lord, I am not worthy for You to come to my humble house. You say a word and that is enough because You are a man of authority. I know what authority is, for I am also a man under authority" (see Luke 7:2-10). As a centurion, he was under the authority of Caesar, and therefore, he had authority over his one hundred men. When he says, "Go," they go; "Come," they come; "Do this," they do it. It cannot be challenged. That is authority.

Our Lord is a man of authority. He says a word and it is done. Now remember, this authority is not His authority as God. As God He says, "Let there be light," and there was light. But here you find, as man He had delegated authority. He just says a word and it is done, says a word and the demon is cast out, says a word and the sea is calmed. He had authority over everything while He was on earth, but as a man, He had no position. While He was exercising His authority, it is spiritual, it is love, it is giving, it is serving. It is because He is a man with authority.

How His authority was challenged! In the beginning of His ministry, our Lord Jesus entered into the temple, and He saw all the trades going on. Our Lord Jesus made a scourge [whip] and drove out all the cattle. He overturned the tables of the moneychangers and He said, "You have made my Father's house a house of merchandise, a bazaar. You have disgraced my Father's house." And the Jews said, "Show us a sign." In other words, on what authority are you doing this? Who are you? Show us a sign. And what sign did our Lord give them? He said, "Destroy this temple, and in three days I will raise it up" (see John 2:13-19). That was the sign.

What is the sign of the authority of our Lord while He was on earth? Giving His life for the world, laying down His life, and taking it up again. That is authority. That is the sign.

At the end of His ministry, it happened again (see Matthew 21:12-13). At His last entry into Jerusalem, after three and a half years of labor, He discovered that the temple was not getting better, but it was getting worse. So again, He cleansed the temple.

After He did that, the chief priests and the elders came and challenged Him: "By what authority do You do this? Who gave You the authority to do this?" They knew that it took authority to do these things, but who gave Him the authority? On whose authority was He doing that? The Lord did not answer that question, but He questioned them, "The baptism of John, whence is it? of heaven or of men?" (Matthew 21:25). In other words, it is clear, it is evident, the Lord does not need to defend His authority.

The Pharisees, the officials of the temple, had position. They were supposed to study the Law and to keep it. Now, in the beginning it might have been because of their godliness. God chose high priests, and those priests were supposed to be set apart to serve God. Maybe in the beginning they had some sincerity, some piety, and because of this they got into a position, but now they had no authority. It was a counterfeit authority based on position, based on tradition, not based on life. So these two authorities clashed: man-made authority (positional and traditional) clashed with real authority (spiritual and life). That false authority only destroys, it never builds; and if it builds, it builds a tower of Babel, a Babylon.

Anyway, it shows that while our Lord was on earth as a man, He had authority. That authority was not God's authority in the first place; that authority was delegated authority. How do we know? In the Gospel according to John, our Lord Jesus said again and again, "I can do nothing of Myself. I saw my Father doing it, so I do it. I cannot say anything on My own. I say it because I heard my Father say it. It is He who is doing it within Me. It is He who is speaking it within Me. I always do the things that please the Father and He is always with Me. If I judge, God has given Me the authority to judge. I judge not on My own, but I judge according to Him."

When our Lord Jesus emptied Himself to become a man, He left His authority as God behind.

He came as a man under authority. He put Himself completely under the authority of God His Father to such an extent that He would never do anything or say anything or go anywhere on His own. Even His timing was in God's hand. You remember how His brothers in the flesh said, "This is the feast time, and everybody is going to Jerusalem. If You want to show Yourself, go to Jerusalem where the people are and show them who You are." And our Lord Jesus said, "Your time is always convenient, but My hour has not yet come" (see John 7:3-6).

In other words, He lived His whole life under God's authority. His obedience to God's authority was so absolute and so perfect, therefore God has given Him delegated authority—perfect and complete. So His authority while He was on earth, was delegated authority. Because He put Himself under God's authority, therefore He was given authority. How He used that authority! He never used His authority for Himself. He always used that authority for His Father's will. He never used His authority to deliver Himself from the cross. He could have done that. When He was mocked and they said, "Come down from the cross and we will believe You," He could very well have done that; but He did not do that. He exercised His authority to remain on the cross. Brothers and sisters, that is delegated authority.

The Principle of God's Delegated Authority

Now, how about us? If God should delegate His authority to us, isn't that a big risk? If God should honor us to delegate His authority to us, remember, it is a tremendous responsibility. To whom will God delegate His authority? To what degree will God delegate His authority to man? The principle is according to the degree of His life in each one of us because authority is in life, in God's life.

Thank God, even though our forefather Adam lost authority, lost the dominion that God gave him, today God again gives authority to those who are His, in whom He has put His own life. With that life comes delegated authority. So every one of us have been given delegated authority. Do you know that? Do you know that every child of God has a measure of delegated authority? It is a tremendous responsibility. He wants you to use that delegated authority to serve God's purpose, to represent God and to do His work. I believe this is the reason He wants to delegate authority. God loves us so much, He wants to honor us so much that He wants us to have a part in His great work, the work of building that holy city, the new Jerusalem, the bride of His beloved Son. You need authority for that. He wants you and me to have a part in it. Therefore He is willing to take that risk with you and me.

Whatever life God has given you, there is that measure of authority there. The Lord says, "Use it under My authority. Exercise it under My authority." When you are doing that, you find God's work is done. There will be building up. But remember one thing: in order to do that, we need to deny ourselves. If our Lord Jesus, who is a perfect man, had to deny Himself every time in the smallest thing as well as the biggest thing, then how much more we, who have this sinful nature in us, need the working of the cross in our lives! If we do not deny ourselves, there is always the danger that we will misuse the authority God has given us. We will use the authority God has given us to misrepresent Him; we will use it for our own purpose; we will use it to build our own kingdom. But remember, it is the kingdom of darkness that we are building. Never for a moment think that because you are given authority, therefore you *become* authority. You are not. No matter how much authority God has given you on the basis of His life in you, whenever you are out of touch with God's life, when you are not living in the Spirit of God, you have no authority whatsoever. You are no authority.

Our trouble today is that authority blinds our eyes. Authority deceives us into thinking that now we *are* authority. So we can say anything we like, we can do anything we want. We can tell people what to do and they must do it; otherwise we punish them. Dear brothers and sisters, this is not the authority of God; this is abuse of God's authority.

We are never the authority. What little authority we may have, it is Christ in us. *He is* the authority.

What is delegated authority? To put it very simply, delegated authority is Christ in you; it is God's life in you. That is delegated authority. That is the measure of authority that you have. Whether you are prophesying according to the proportion of faith, or you are serving according to the measure God has given you, do not be out of bounds (see Romans 12:6-7). Do not be careless, thinking that now you are the authority. You never are.

So, brother Nee told us there are three requirements for being delegated authority. Number one: always remember that God is the authority and nobody else. Number two: always deny yourself because you are to represent God's authority, not to substitute God's authority. Number three: always stay in communion with God because when you are out of touch with God, you lose that authority and what authority you still claim to have is a counterfeit.

Being Under Authority

Now we come to this matter of being under authority. It is equally difficult to be in authority and to be under authority. Do not think that to be in authority is easy. It is very difficult; probably, it is more difficult than being under authority. Now there is no problem to be under the authority of God directly. Our problem is in being under delegated authority because we will say, "Who are you? You are not God. Why should I submit to you?" It is because we do not understand what authority is. Brothers and sisters, if we understand what authority is, there is no problem because whether it is direct or delegated, it is God. When we are submitting to the authority that God has set above us, we are not submitting to men or women, we are submitting to God. If only we can see this, then where is the problem? Our problem is with God; it is not with man. So, if we have that problem, we should go to God and deal with it. Do not try to deal with man because you will not be able to solve it. We have to go to God to solve that problem.

As a matter of fact, I love that verse: "Submitting yourselves to one another in the fear of Christ" (Ephesians 5:21). Oh, I love that verse. Paul was going to tell us about the relationship between husband and wife, the relationship between parents and children, the relationship between masters and slaves. In other words, he was going to tell us that in this world, there is an order. In this world, there are those who will be put in authority and there will be those who will be under authority. That is the way God has arranged this world, either nationally, or in a home, or in the church. Before he mentioned that, he laid down a principle: "Submitting yourselves to one another in the fear of Christ."

Dear brothers and sisters, our first thought should not be, "Whom will I have authority over?" Our first thought should be, "Whom should I submit to?" Here we find, submission should be our attitude. We should seek for submission, not seek for authority. Submit to one another in the fear of Christ. In other words, as the members of the body of Christ, every member has a measure of Christ, and to that measure of Christ, we must submit. It is in the fear of Christ, and "the fear" there is not the fear of punishment. The fear there is the fear of not pleasing the Lord. We want to please the Lord, and because we want to please Him so much, therefore, whenever we see that measure, that expression, that manifestation of Christ coming out from any brother or sister, we submit to it. Sometimes, the great member has to submit to the small member. Submit yourselves to one another in the fear of Christ. If this is our attitude what will happen? When we submit ourselves one to another, then the divine order will appear. The divine order appears through our submission. When we submit ourselves to one another, the Spirit of God will show us whom He has set up as authority over us to obey and to whom we should learn to submit. That will come out very naturally.

In the church today, the reason there is so much quarrel over this matter of leadership or who is to be in authority, is because everybody wants to be in authority and not to submit. Everyone wants others to submit to them and not to submit to others. That is the problem. So when you are doing that, remember the divine order will never come forth. Whenever brothers and sisters really see it and have an attitude of submitting to one another in the fear of Christ, God will decide who should be in authority. Do not look at the "Adam" and the "Eve" in your brothers and sisters, but look at the Christ in them. Try to find Christ in them and submit to the Christ in them. When everyone is doing that, God will decide who should be in authority.

To be in authority is a tremendous responsibility; it is to serve as the bondslave of all. Now who wants to do that? Unless God apprehends you, who wants to do that? But when God apprehends you, how dare you not do it? It is for God, not for yourself. It is to desire a good work, the work of God to be done. And I believe with my whole heart that the order will be manifested supernaturally naturally, so that should be no problem. Our whole attitude needs to be changed.

There is much more that we can share, but our time is up. We do trust the Holy Spirit of God to show us what authority is, and if we really know what authority is, submission and obedience should be no problem. Again I say, naturally, we know neither authority nor obedience. It is not in us. Whether it is authority, it is Christ; whether it is obedience, it is Christ. He is the very principle of authority; He is the very principle of obedience. And it is Christ in us who enables us to have delegated authority. It is Christ in us who enables us to submit to the authorities that God has set above us.

Questions On Spiritual Authority

Question #1—What does it mean to give absolute obedience and absolute submission to God, while giving man absolute submission but not absolute obedience?

This statement needs to be clarified. It is clear that our God is sovereign. He is perfect and therefore His authority is absolute. To His absolute authority our response can be nothing but absolute submission and absolute obedience. Again, we say that submission is our attitude; it is an inward attitude; and obedience is an action, our outward act. To God, who is the authority—absolute, unlimited, and perfect—we have to give absolute submission and absolute obedience. This is not merely doing something outwardly to express that we are obeying what He wants us to do, but even in our hearts there needs to be that absolute submission. I think there is no question about this.

The problem is with man. When man is given authority, when authority has been delegated to him, what should be our response to man? If God, in His sovereignty, should put someone above us, what should be our response to the authorities God has set above us? In Romans 13:1 it says very clearly, "Let every soul be subject to the authorities that are above him." So we need to subject ourselves to the authorities God has put over us, but to what extent? If, in God's providence, He has delegated authorities and we are being placed under such authorities, as far as our inward attitude is concerned, we need to have submission because it is God who put us there. We need to submit to such authorities. We submit not only for the sake of law, but also for the sake of conscience. As far as our submission is concerned, it can be absolute; that is, we will not rebel, we will not rise up against, but in our inward spirit we are willing to submit. With man, however, no matter who he is, we can only give absolute submission, that is our attitude, but we can never give absolute obedience. Our obedience to man is relative, although our submission can be absolute. It is because man is not perfect and, oftentimes, man may misuse the authority God has given him. Oftentimes, it is not God's authority at all, it is position and because of this, we find that we have a higher authority that we have to obey. So whenever man's authority, so-called, conflicts with God's authority, then we have to obey God rather than man.

We have many instances of this in the Bible, not only in the Old Testament, but also in the New Testament. For instance, when the children of Israel were in Egypt, Pharaoh gave orders to the midwives to kill every male baby. However, the midwives preserved the lives of these children because they had to obey a higher authority. In another instance, Moses' parents disobeyed Pharaoh by keeping the baby for three months because they saw that the baby was very fair (see Exodus 1).

In the New Testament, when the apostles were brought before the council, which is the highest Jewish authority, they were forbidden to preach in the name of the Lord Jesus. And they said, "Whether to obey man or to obey God, you can decide yourself, but what we have seen and heard, we have to preach" (see Acts 4:19-20). Later on, they stated even more positively that they had to obey God rather than man. When man and God are in conflict, we can give to a man who is above us absolute submission but not absolute obedience, because the latter we have to give to God. In other words, when Peter and John and the apostles said this, they did not say it in a spirit of rebellion; they said it in the spirit of meekness: "We will not rise up against you, but we have to obey God and we are willing to take the consequences. If you want to put us in jail, we will go to jail gladly." That shows that there is absolute submission, but relative obedience.

Question #2 — In prehistoric times, when God delegated His authority to the angelic beings, Lucifer rebelled against God's authority. He turned himself into Satan, adversary of God. Did he lose the delegated authority God had given him or did he still retain some or all of that authority?

I can only give you my thoughts on this and I struggled with this matter even before I came to the conference. Let us define authority: Authority is the right to exercise power. God is *the* authority of the universe; all authority comes from God. So I feel when a person or an angel is not under God's authority, then the delegated authority is gone. In other words, he has lost the right to exercise the power given to him. The power is there but the authority is not there. There is a difference between authority and power. Authority is the right to do things, and we have only the right to do God's will. If we are not under God's authority, what right do we have? That spiritual authority, the delegated authority of God, is no longer there. It is being substituted by a false authority and that false authority is man's authority, or it is a positional authority.

We mentioned in the very beginning that position comes from spiritual life and because of that spiritual life, there is such a position. But when there is rebellion and the delegated authority is gone, when that spirituality is not there, that position becomes a false position and it has to be maintained by a false authority, backed up by power; and that is where all the problems come from.

Question #3—Does Satan have authority and is it really his?

This question asks whether Satan still retains some of the original authority he received, or if he received the authority from man.

When Satan tempted our Lord Jesus in the wilderness, he tempted the Lord by showing Him all the glory of the kingdoms and the riches of the world. He did not say, "This earth is mine, it is given to me. I have the right to give it to whomever I want." No. He said, "The kingdoms of the world, this power and their glory are given to me. If You bow to me, I will give them to You." In Darby's translation of Luke, it says, "They have been given up to me" (see Luke 4:6-7).

Satan became the ruler of this world. Now the world is a system that Satan organized and controlled when man submitted himself to Satan. In other words, this earth still belongs to God; the right is still God's right. He has not given up that right. He only waits for a time when that right will be exercised. Our Lord Jesus, as the risen Lord, began to exercise that right, that authority, to bring the whole world back to God, that all the kingdoms of the world should become the kingdoms of our Lord and of His Christ (see Revelation 11:15b). So, I feel that when angels or men are not under the authority of God, the delegated authority is gone and you find substitutions; but the power is still there, and that is the problem.

Question #4—If the authority is a false one, do we need to submit ourselves?

When you read Romans chapter 13, it is very clear that all authorities are set up by God. If we resist authority, we resist the ordinance of God and bring judgment to ourselves. Now why is this so? Brothers and sisters, it is because this whole world system is wrong. Authority is wrong, position is wrong, everything is wrong, and we are living in this wrong environment. What can we do? Since everything is wrong, what should we do? Should we be wrong too? That is where the glory of the gospel comes in. Our Lord Jesus not only restored obedience, but also authority. He restored God's original concept of authority and of obedience. By restoring these things, He becomes the Author of our eternal salvation. That is to say, He is restoring both authority and obedience in His church. Therefore, He brings us back to the beginning.

When the Pharisees challenged the Lord about divorce, they said, "Moses allowed us to have divorce" and the Lord's answer was, "In the beginning it was not so" (see Matthew 19:8-9). We find that with the salvation of the Lord, He always brings us to the very beginning, which is the beginning of the meaning of authority and obedience. So in the beginning, when God delegated authority, it was His authority, but because of the sin of the world a change has come in. Instead of representing God, the authority misrepresents God. Even though it misrepresents God, it has to pretend that it is still representing Him because no government will announce that evil is good. It will try to explain evil as good, but no government can ever announce that evil is good. It still has to maintain that good is good and evil is evil. In other words, you have to pretend that you are still representing God, even though in reality it is not true; it is a façade, a pretense. That is the reason why it says in Romans chapter 13 that you have to subject yourselves to the authorities because they are God's servants. They do not bear the sword in vain; they are to punish the evil and to reward the good. Now at least with all false authorities, they have to pretend that they are doing this. It is not until the son of lawlessness appears that he will come out and say, "Evil is good."

Question #5—Even though the authorities God has set up in this world are no longer according to His original thought, God is still working to restore authority and obedience. While He is working, He allows these things to continue for a time. Since we are in that kind of situation, what should we do?

We do not try to restore authority and obedience by being disobedient. We try to restore authority and obedience by being submissive. In other words, if God has put that authority over us providentially, He allows it and He is still working. He has not finished yet, and we should manifest what real obedience is and what real authority is. That is the reason why we still need to submit to the authorities that are above us. God has sovereignly put us there. We need to be submissive; but again, it is not absolute obedience. Obedience is relative. We have to obey God rather than man.

Sometimes we say that we can obey a man to the extent of our conscience. When it touches our conscience, then we have to stop because conscience is the voice of God. We have to obey God rather than man. We can be submissive, and we are willing to take the consequences of not obeying. I think this is a very difficult area, but the principle is clear. When God is working toward the recovery of authority and obedience, we have to learn how to submit in order to restore the right authority and the right obedience. So, in a sense, by doing so, we are working with God. Eventually, all these false authorities will be cast aside, and all authority will be of God. "Thine is the kingdom, the authority, and the glory forever."

At the time our Lord Jesus was on earth, the authority God allowed over the Jewish people was a false authority; it was the Roman Empire. But even though it was the Roman Empire, we have to say that God set up that authority. We find it even in Daniel's prophecy. Our Lord Jesus lived under that false authority and our Lord never rebelled against the Roman Empire. The Jewish people were expecting the Messiah to come and overturn the Roman Empire, the yoke that was upon them, and set them free, making them the first nation of the world. When they discovered that our Lord was not doing that, they despised Him, they rejected Him, and they crucified Him. But the Lord said, "Give to Caesar what belongs to Caesar and to God what belongs to God." He even paid tribute to Caesar. Our Lord is a good example to us. We have to obey the authorities that God has put over us, but there is a degree of obedience.

The same is true for a family. The parents are the authority God has set over us and we need to obey them. We obey them to the extent that their command does not conflict with God's command.

The same thing is true in the church. God may raise up some people to function as elders and they represent the government of God in the church. But again, when they are not under God's authority, then they have no authority whatsoever to command us to do things. When that happens, we can submit, or have a submissive attitude, but we do not need to do what they command us to do because we have to obey God. So there is a limit; it is not an unlimited authority.

Our problem is not only in the world, but also in the church. Whenever that real spiritual authority is no longer there and it is substituted by man's authority who tries to maintain that position, then, I think we need to understand that we can give absolute submission but relative obedience.

Question #6—What should be done if, in the church, a person gets very authoritative and dictatorial?

If we read the word of God, we will find that God has already safe-guarded against such situations because God has never set up one person to represent His authority in the church. To put it in another way, He has never delegated authority to one person as the head in the church—never! Our Lord Jesus is the Head of the church. He may delegate authority to man, but He is still the Head of the church. He has not given up all of His authority yet. He may delegate authority, but He does not give up His authority. Even when He delegates His authority, it is limited; it is not absolute. Otherwise, God would let out His authority and He would have no authority whatsoever. The Lord still is the authority, but He will delegate authority in a limited way and not only in a limited way, but in a corporate way.

The word *elder* in the Bible is never in the singular number; it is always plural in number. For the sake of the work of God, we have to have some people who will take responsibility for the whole church, and they are in plural number—the "elders," not elder. If it is one person, it is very dangerous because that one person could substitute someone other than Christ as the head. But if it is plurality, then there is no one who can be a substitute Christ. Also, in plurality there is a kind of mutuality. There are checks and balances. These people who function as elders check and balance one another so that none will try to lay claim to being *the* authority. Instead, each will learn to submit to the other, and as they submit to one another, then the authority of God as the Head is manifested. So the scriptures actually safe-guard against such situations.

Unfortunately, very early in church history, even in the second century, the idea began to change. Some people with more ability or more ambition began to try to dominate, and the idea of the bishop being over the elders began to come in. Gradually, the bishop idea, or the presiding elder idea began to become popular—one person takes the front seat, and the others just follow him.

Now, these ideas came from man not from God. If we follow the word of God, there should be no such thing; and yet, even in the scriptures there is one case. The third epistle of John deals with this situation. John wrote to Gaius that in the church where he was, there was one man, Diotrephes, who tried to dominate, rule and overrule everything. Even when the apostle wrote a letter of recommendation, he rejected it, and if anyone should receive those visiting brothers, Diotrephes would cast them out. Unfortunately, in history, there are such cases. When they do occur, how are you going to deal with them? In III John, the apostle John said, "I will come and face the situation and deal with it." Such situations can only be dealt with by spiritual authority; false authority can only be dealt with by true authority.

Now, what should the brothers and sisters do if the apostle did not come? John instructed and said, "You do what you have been doing—receiving the brothers. That is the right thing to do." In other words, you have to disobey the one who claims to be the authority because it is not God's authority. You have to obey God and do the things that God has called you to do. Also, brothers and sisters should deal with this situation in a spiritual way and that is through prayer. Through prayer, God will either change that person or remove that person.

Question #7—When you find a situation like the above, or when the leadership is not doing what it should do, then what should you do?

Should we run out and find another fellowship of a kind that we like and join them? What should we do? The whole matter concerns one thing: Do we understand what the church is, what a local church really represents?

Oftentimes, we talk about the local church, but we do not really know what the local church is. What is the church? If it is the church, there is no way to run out of the church. If it is the local church, there is no way to run out of it because the church is the body of Christ. How can we run out of that? How can we change our fellowship? There is no way to do that. So, first of all, we need to know what the church really is. There are so many who claim to be the church who are not the church.

That is unfortunate. If we can see the difference, then I think we can answer this question.

If the fellowship is recognized before God as His church, as a lampstand before Him, then we have to remain there even if there are weaknesses and problems. By patience, by faith, by prayer, by faithfulness, we need to look to the Lord that the Lord will recover or do something. But if it is not the church in the sight of God, or if it has changed its nature so much that the lampstand has been removed, even though physically it is still there, then, brothers and sisters, it is time to get out. But the problem is not in getting out, the problem is with whom should we meet? That is the problem. So we really need to know what the church is and then we will be able to join with those who serve the Lord with a pure heart, seeking the Lord with a pure heart. We can join ourselves with them and stay with them for the testimony of Jesus. It is really a matter of understanding. It is not a matter of when you are unhappy, then you can go somewhere else. It is a matter of really seeing what the Lord is after.

Part Two: Spiritual House

The Meaning of The House

I Peter 2:5—Yourselves also, as living stones, are being built up a spiritual house, a holy priesthood, to offer spiritual sacrifices acceptable to God by Jesus Christ.

Genesis 28:10-22—And Jacob went out from Beer-sheba, and went towards Haran. And he lighted on a certain place, and lodged there, because the sun had set. And he took [one] of the stones of the place, and made [it] his pillow, and lay down in that place. And he dreamed, and behold, a ladder was set up on the earth, and the top of it reached to the heavens. And behold, angels of God ascended and descended upon it. And behold, Jehovah stood above it. And he said, I am Jehovah, the God of Abraham, thy father, and the God of Isaac: the land on which thou liest, to thee will I give it, and to thy seed. And thy seed shall be as the dust of the earth, and thou shalt spread abroad to the west, and to the east, and to the north, and to the south; and in thee and in thy seed shall all the families of the earth be blessed. And behold, I am with thee, and will keep thee in all [places] to which thou goest, and will bring thee again into this land; for I will not leave thee until I have done what I have spoken to thee of. And Jacob awoke from his sleep, and said, Surely Jehovah is in this place, and I knew [it] not. And he was afraid, and said, How dreadful is this place! this is none other but the house of God, and this is the gate of heaven. And Jacob rose early in the morning, and took the stone that he had made his pillow, and set it up [for] a pillar, and poured oil on the top of it. And he called the name of that place Beth-el; but the name of that city was Luz at the first. And Jacob vowed a vow, saying, If God will be with me, and keep me on this road that I go, and will give me bread to eat, and a garment to put on, and I come again to my father's house in peace—then shall Jehovah be my God. And this stone, which I have set up [for] a pillar, shall be God's house; and of all that thou wilt give me I will without fail give the tenth to thee.

Revelation 21:1-7—And I saw a new heaven and a new earth; for the first heaven and the first earth had passed away, and the sea exists no more.

And I saw the holy city, new Jerusalem, coming down out of the heaven from God, prepared as a bride adorned for her husband. And I heard a loud voice out of the heaven, saying, Behold, the tabernacle of God [is] with men, and he shall tabernacle with them, and they shall be his people, and God himself shall be with them, their God. And he shall wipe away every tear from their eyes; and death shall not exist any more, nor grief, nor cry, nor distress shall exist any more, for the former things have passed away. And he that sat on the throne said, Behold, I

make all things new. And he says [to me], Write,
for these words are true and faithful. And he said
to me, It is done. I am the Alpha and the Omega,
the beginning and the end. I will give to him that
thirsts of the fountain of the water of life freely.
He that overcomes shall inherit these things, and
I will be to him God, and he shall be to me son.

The theme God has given us for this time is *Spiritual House*. We are actually touching upon the eternal purpose of God. God has a purpose which He purposed in His beloved Son, and He purposed that even before the foundation of the world. And what He has purposed for Himself in His Son is a house, a dwelling place, a home.

God created the heavens and the earth, but these are not His home, His house, His dwelling place. His desire is to dwell among men and that is the reason why you and I were created. He created man to fulfill that longing of His heart. He wants to dwell among man. He wants to make man His eternal home that man may also find their eternal home in Him. This is God's purpose.

As we touch upon this matter of spiritual house we have a problem because we are so familiar with all these things. We are familiar with God's house; we are familiar with the church of God. Because all these things are so familiar to us, I am afraid we have lost that cutting edge, that conviction, that commitment which is necessary when we touch upon the eternal purpose of God. So our prayer is

that the Lord will enable us to forget all that we
have known in the past about the house, the dwelling place, the church. Now let's forget everything
that we have known and let us each just come to
Him as a little child that we may receive living revelation from Him and really be drawn into the purpose of God and be part of it.

The house God is after is not a physical one. Unfortunately, that is always what we think He desires. He wants a spiritual house. He can only
dwell in a spiritual house because the heaven and
the heaven of heavens cannot contain Him. He is
too big for the physical universe. And He is Spirit,
so what He desires is a spiritual house, and He
wants to find that house in man. You can see right
away that man has to be spiritual in order to be His
house. That is the reason why in Isaiah it is said,
"But to this man will I look: to the afflicted and
contrite in spirit, and who trembleth at my word"
(Isaiah 66:2b). It is not just any kind of man; it is
spiritual man that God wants to build His spiritual
house.

Jacob and the House of God
Union and Communion

The first mention of the house of God is found
in Genesis chapter 28. I believe we are familiar
with the story. Jacob, that twister, stole not only the
birthright, but also the blessing of the firstborn
from his brother, and because of this he had to flee

for his life. He was in the wilderness and the sun was setting, so he took a stone and made it a pillow to lay his head upon. Now, that very picture will show you how miserable, how pitiful, how sad the situation was. Yet the first mention of the house of God was revealed in this most unlikely place—the desert. It was revealed to the most unlikely person—Jacob, the supplanter. It was revealed under the most unlikely environment—because Jacob was homeless, fleeing from his brother and his home. So I do feel that it is not because of what we are that God reveals His house to us. It is the mercy of God that He should reveal His house to His people, not because we deserve it. It is all of God's mercy.

Jacob dreamed a dream, and in that dream He saw a ladder set up and reaching to heaven. God was stationed there at the top of the ladder. Jacob was sleeping at the foot of the ladder; the angels of God were ascending and descending (very busy), upon that ladder, and God spoke to Jacob. This is the first revelation of the house of God.

What is the house of God? The house of God is the union and communion of God and man in Christ Jesus. That is the house of God. Today, we know what that ladder is because you remember in John 1:51 our Lord Jesus said:

> Verily, verily, I say to you, Henceforth ye shall see the heaven opened, and the angels of God ascending and descending on the Son of man.

Nathaniel, that honest Jew, was led to the Lord, but he could not believe that anything good could come out of Nazareth. Yet when the Lord saw him, He said, "I saw you under that fig tree." Now strangely, when the Lord said, "I saw you under that fig tree," immediately Nathaniel said, "My Lord, my God." Why? It is because he was a true Israelite. Evidently, under the fig tree he was dreaming about that kingdom because the fig tree is a type of Israel. He was longing for that kingdom to come, the Messianic Kingdom. So when the Lord said, "I saw you under that fig tree," the Lord really spoke to his heart and immediately he realized that this is the Messiah. But the Lord said, "You are going to see something bigger." Nathaniel was only thinking of the Messianic Kingdom. That is big, yes, but there is something bigger than that. The Lord said, "You shall see the angels ascending and descending upon the Son of Man" (see John 1:43-51).

Here you find that ladder; it is the Son of Man. He who is the Son of God, He who is equal with God, He who is in the form of God, emptied Himself and took upon Himself the form of a slave, even the fashion of a man. He came into this world to become the Son of Man. Why? Because He was to be that ladder. He is the One who is to connect earth with heaven and heaven with earth. He is the One who is to bring God and man, man and God together. He is the only way that we can come to God; He is the only way that God can come to us.

And not only does He bring God and man together, but you find there is a communion between man and God.

The angels were ascending and descending on that ladder. We know angels are ministering servants; they minister God to man, and they minister man to God. In other words, you find that through the work of the angels, they are trying to bring what Christ has done for us into our life. So the first meaning of the house of God is the coming together of God and man in Christ Jesus, the union of life with God, the communion that God and man will have.

God stationed Himself at the top of the ladder and spoke to Jacob. He said, "I am the God of Abraham, your father, and the God of Isaac. The place that you sleep now will be yours. I will bless you and your seed shall be as the dust of the earth, and the land east, west, north, and south shall all be given to you. And in thee and in thy seed all the families of the nations shall be blessed. I will be with you until all that I have said shall be done" (see Genesis 28:13-15).

Here you find God is the giver. He is giving everything, and Jacob is the receiver; he is the one receiving. But unfortunately, after God had spoken to him, he woke up and said, "Surely Jehovah is in this place, and I knew it not." And he was afraid, and said, "How dreadful is this place!" (Genesis 28:16b-17a).

In a sense, Jacob knew that he was not fit for God. God is holy and yet look at Jacob—what a person he was! So when that revelation was given to him, it was a surprise. He did not know that God was present there with him. Who would think that God would be with such a person? Yet God was there, and Jacob felt that it was a dreadful place.

Today, when we talk about the house of God, we feel so good, so comfortable, so peaceful. I think that is our problem, because if we can really see "how dreadful is this place," there is hope. We make it too common, as if the presence of God is nothing. The presence of God demands a lot and Jacob knew it. He knew he was totally unfit for God. God came to him and he was afraid, yet he knew that was the house of God. God wanted to be with man. God wanted to be drawn together even with Jacob. He knew that and he said, "This is the house of God, the gate of heaven."

But how did Jacob react to this great revelation of the house of God? Jacob was so limited by his petty self. In a sense, you can see that Jacob just could not rise above himself. How did Jacob respond? On the one hand, he understood: this is the house of God. God is after a house. God wants to be united with man through Christ Jesus. He knew that God was desiring communion with man. He knew all these things. He knew that was what it was all about, and yet on the other hand, he just could not take it in; he could not understand, he could not rise above himself. He was Jacob. So he began to bargain with God.

Now, you may say Jacob did not believe in God and what God had said, but I think he did. The problem was that he was so confined by his own self. God gave him great promises and yet he bargained with God for little things because that is all he understood. He said, "If..." He could not trust anybody. He could not even trust God. So he said: "Now You have given me all these great promises. All right, *if* You give me food to eat, *if* You give me a garment to put on, *if* You will lead me peacefully back home, then I will make You my God, and I will take this stone that I made as my pillow and set it up as a pillar to be Thy house, and I will give You one tenth of all that I have."

He was thinking all of himself. He did not understand that the revelation of God's house is for God. He was self-centered, not God-centered. He was interested only in himself, his own welfare. He was not interested in God's interest. He was so limited by himself that even if God gave him food to eat, garments to put on, and eventually led him safely home, he said, "This pillar shall be Thy house." In other words, you find he was only thinking of the physical as if God wanted a physical house. He did not understand that God wanted to make Jacob His house. And in order to make Jacob His house God had to transform Jacob into Israel. It is not so much what Jacob would do to build God a house (as a matter of fact a pillar is not a

house). It is not his service. It is God who is working for that house in Jacob by transforming him
into Israel so that God can be united with him in
life and also there can be that communion together. Jacob did not understand that.

But thank God, after God had dealt with that
man Jacob, twenty some years later, he went back
to Bethel (see Genesis 35). He called this place *Bethel*, the "house of God." Eventually, he went back to
Bethel and built an altar there. He called that place
El Bethel, the "God of the house of God." An altar
is an expression of communion, so finally, Jacob
began to understand what God was really after in
his life. God wants a house of union and
communion.

Now, we laugh at Jacob but how about ourselves? Do we have a revelation of the house of
God? Or are we so wrapped up with ourselves that
even if that revelation is given, we do not understand. Maybe mentally we do have some idea that
this is the house of God, the gate of heaven, and
yet actually in our lives we are all wrapped up
with ourselves. We are still interested in our own
interests, and we bargain with God and say: "If
throughout my life You give me food to eat, garments to wear, and give me peace and security,
then I will make You my God and I will serve You.
I will build You a house, a physical one."

Brothers and sisters, is this not what we are doing today? Do we really understand what the
house of God is? Do we know that what He is re-

ally after is not what we can do for Him, but God is really after *us*? Do we understand that in order for this house to be a reality He has to do much work in our lives? He has to transform us from Jacob—we are all Jacob—into *Israel*, "prince with God." Do we understand that He is longing for communion with us, union with us in Christ Jesus? I wonder. We need to be delivered out of ourselves. We need to be delivered from our self-centeredness. We need to be delivered from self-interest in order to really enter into the house of God that He is after. So, I do feel that it is a time for us to reconsider before the Lord whether we really understand what the house of God is.

As Jacob, are we fit to be one with God in Christ Jesus? Do we realize that there is so much in us, almost all in us, that needs to be drastically dealt with before we can be fit to be His house? Do we understand that what He longs for is communion? It is not what we can do for Him. How many of us are busily serving Him, doing what we call Christian work, involved in many activities, building the church, planting the church, and so on? Is this what God is really after, or is it that He is after a time with us? "Mary has chosen the better part" (see Luke 10:42). This is the house of God. So first of all, the house of God is the union and communion of God and man in Christ Jesus. That is the house of God.

The Tabernacle
Communication, Worship, and Service

And Jehovah spoke to Moses, saying, Speak unto the children of Israel, that they bring me a heave-offering: of every one whose heart prompteth him, ye shall take my heave-offering...

And they shall make me a sanctuary, that I may dwell among them. According to all that I shall shew thee, the pattern of the tabernacle, and the pattern of all the utensils thereof, even so shall ye make it...

And thou shalt put the mercy-seat above on the ark, and shalt put in the ark the testimony that I shall give thee. And there will I meet with thee, and will speak with thee from above the mercy-seat, from between the two cherubim which are upon the ark of the testimony, everything that I will give thee in commandment unto the children of Israel. (Exodus 25:1, 8-9, 21-22)

Secondly, when you come to this matter of the house of God, you find the tabernacle. After God delivered the children of Israel out of Egypt, He brought them to Mount Sinai. Now, when He delivered them out of Egypt, He did not tell them why He delivered them, what His purpose was in delivering them. But after He brought them to Mount Sinai, there He revealed to them not only the Ten Commandments but also the tabernacle. Unfortunately today, we know more about the Ten

Commandments than the tabernacle, as if God revealed nothing but the Ten Commandments on Mount Sinai. Actually, God did reveal the Ten Commandments to the children of Israel as His testimony, as the law given to His people.

However, even more, after God had given the Ten Commandments, the testimony, the law, He revealed to Moses the pattern of the tabernacle. He said, "Let the people give a heave-offering." A heave-offering is a love offering. In other words, it is not something forced, but rather it is something you give out of love. With a redeemed people, God asked for a love offering. As a matter of fact, we who are redeemed are bought with a price, even with the blood of our Lord Jesus. We are no longer our own; we are God's. We belong to Him and He has every right to demand that we give offerings to Him. But that is not the way God works because if He did it in that way He would never have His house. So with a house in view, even with the redeemed people, God never deals with us in a legalistic way. God always deals with us in love. So God said, "You are redeemed, I have brought you out of slavery. You are a free people. Now, out of your free will, you give. For what purpose? That you may make Me a sanctuary, a house, a tabernacle that I may dwell among you."

So, the purpose of redemption is God's dwelling with His people. That is the purpose. The children of Israel were slaves for so long and suddenly they got their freedom. Once they were free, they may have thought: "Now we can do what we could not do in the past. Now we can have our heart's desire. Now we can live our own life. Formerly, we were slaves, we had no rights; we could not do what we wanted to do; we could not have what we wanted to have. Now we are free, and not only free, but when we got out, we actually deprived Egypt of her wealth. Now we have all this gold and silver and all these things. What a life we can live now for ourselves!"

Suppose the children of Israel had thought in that way. Now God said: "Wait a minute; that is not the purpose of My delivering you. The reason I delivered you out of slavery is because I want to dwell among you. I want to be with you. That is My purpose."

Brothers and sisters, isn't that true with us today? We who are bought with a price, the Lord never demands that we should give ourselves to Him as a living sacrifice. The Lord said that it has to be a heave-offering; it has to be a love-offering. "I beseech you therefore, brethren, by the mercies of God, that ye present your bodies a living sacrifice, holy, acceptable unto God, which is your reasonable service, [or your spiritual worship]" (Romans 12:1 KJV).

So God said, "Give me a heave-offering." Why do we need to present our bodies a living sacrifice? It is because God wants to dwell among us. He wants to use what we have offered to build a sanctuary, a holy place for Himself and also for us. That is the purpose.

When God gave that pattern to Moses, on the one hand, it is as if God said: "You cannot approach Me. I am holy. You are unclean, you are unholy, you are sinful. Even though you are redeemed, you are still defiled. You cannot approach Me."

Therefore, you find the approach to God is quite elaborate; it is not simple. You have to go through the brazen altar. You have to go through the laver for washing. You have to go through the holy place—the candlestick, the shewbread, the altar of incense, and then there is a veil. No one can enter. Only the high priest can go in to make atonement once a year with blood and smoke and quickly withdraw. In other words, the way to the holiest was not open.

So when you read about the tabernacle, you get the impression that God is so holy, and who are we that we can draw near to Him? We cannot. It is difficult, very difficult. And yet on the other hand, you find that God gave the tabernacle to man because it shows God's longing for communication, God's longing for fellowship with man. You get a very mixed feeling in your heart. And isn't that true? God longs to communicate with people. In the tabernacle, in the holiest of all is the ark, and in the ark is the testimony, and on the cover of the ark is the mercy seat. And God said: "I will speak to you between the cherubim on the mercy seat. All that I will command to you I will speak to you. You will meet with Me, and you will speak to Me" (see Exodus 25:22).

What is the house of God? The house of God is a place of communication. (I am thinking less of the physical building but more of the people in the house—a home.) Now what is a home? A home is more than just a building of brick or wood or even mud and straw. No, a home is those who are in that house who are communicating with one another. That makes it a home.

Suppose you have a family of maybe four people or eight people and there is no communication between the father and the mother, no communication between the parents and the children, no communication between the brothers and the sisters. There is no communication. They all live there in that house but there is no speaking. Everybody is quiet, silent, glaring at each other. Do you call this a home?

What is the tabernacle? The tabernacle is a meeting place where God and man meet, that God may speak to man and man may speak to God. That is the house of God. Of course, in the Old Testament time it was very difficult. There was the outer court, the holy place, the veil, and then the holiest of all. We know of course that the ark is a type of Christ, and the law of God, God's testimony, can only be kept in Christ.

We remember when the law was given, the children of Israel said: "All that God has said we will do. We do not even need to hear directly from God. It is good enough for us to hear indirectly and we will keep everything that God has said." But before the two tables of stone reached them they had already broken the law. In other words, nobody can keep the law. The law is kept only in Christ Jesus. He is the end of all laws. But thank God, He not only kept the laws of God, but we find the ark was covered with the mercy seat. Christ has fulfilled all righteousness and on the basis of that, God in Christ can show mercy to us.

Today, we are in such a better position because Christ has already come. He is our mercy seat. The veil is broken, is rent. There is nothing standing between, so our communication, our communion, our fellowship with God can be uninterrupted. This is our position today. In Christ Jesus we can have uninterrupted communion with God. God is able to speak to us and we are able to speak to God. There is communication between God and us and that makes the house of God. Hebrews 3:5-6 says:

> And Moses indeed was faithful in all his house, as a ministering servant, for a testimony of the things to be spoken after; but Christ, as Son over his house, whose house are we, if indeed we hold fast the boldness and the boast of hope firm to the end.

Here we find that we are His house if indeed we hold fast the boldness and the boast of hope firm to the end. "Wherefore, even as says the Holy Spirit, To-day if ye will hear his voice, harden not your hearts" (Hebrews 3:7).

Are we the house of God? We are if we hear Him. Our God is a God who speaks. Not only has He spoken in the past to our fathers through the prophets in many ways and in many forms, but in the last days He has spoken to us in His Son (see Hebrews 1:1-2). There is a voice coming out from the mercy seat incessantly. God is speaking in His Son continuously to us, but do we hear? We say we are the house of God, but do we hear His voice? Individually, are we hearing Him? Will a day pass without hearing a word from Him? Is it possible? Is it normal? Or if we have heard, do we harden our hearts and not obey?

Brothers and sisters, I am thinking that today we are almost like the time of Eli, because you remember in I Samuel it says that during the time of Eli the judge, "… the word of God was rare, and the vision was infrequent" (see 3:1). Is that the normal condition of God's relationship with His people, His redeemed people? God cannot speak to the world today because they will not listen. Even if God speaks, they say it thunders. They do not understand, they cannot hear the voice. But the church today is the redeemed of the Lord. And here you find God's words were rare; God rarely spoke, and He rarely appeared to His people, very infrequently. Can that represent the house of God? Do we hear the voice of our Lord every day? He that has ears let him hear what the Spirit says to the churches, but the churches are not listening. Our condition has forced God into silence.

Even worse, you find that after Malachi, the last prophet, for four hundred years God was silent. He could not speak. How it saddened His heart. What if you are parents and for one day you are forced to be kept quiet? You cannot say anything to your children because if you say something, probably, there will be an uproar, or a rebellion. Think of that. Can you call that a home?

However, this is what is happening today. We are not listening. We harden our hearts. How we need to repent and really be before the Lord. How we need to pray that the Lord will give us a hearing heart that we may hear Him every day! He will speak to us. (I am not thinking of audible voices; sometimes God does.) But more so He will speak through His Spirit who dwells in our spirit. The reason why we do not hear Him is because we are so far away from Him. We are occupied with so many things. We hear so many voices that we cannot hear Him. Oh, we need to have a tender heart, a heart that is turned towards Him. And I do believe that if our hearts are turned towards Him we cannot fail to hear Him speaking. He loves to talk with us. He loves to communicate what is in His heart to us. He is shut up to Himself. He longs to share His burden with us. He longs to share what is in His heart with us. But where are the people who are ready to receive His burden? But we are not interested.

More than that He wants us to communicate with Him. He wants us to draw near to Him, not because we are worthy in our righteousness. No, never. It is because Christ is our righteousness and through our Lord Jesus we have ready access to Him. And He wants us to go to Him to talk to Him, to converse with Him, to communicate, to tell Him everything that is in our heart; pour ourselves out to Him.

Today, we find people are very lonely because they have no one to talk to. But here is your heavenly Father, always waiting with patience, love, and sympathy to hear what you want to say to Him. And why don't you want to do it? This makes it the house of God. Individually, this is so; corporately it is so. The church should hear the voice of the Spirit. When the church does not hear what the Spirit of God is saying, something is very wrong. The church ought to be a place where you can bring everything to Him. So this is the second meaning of the house of God.

The tabernacle is a place of service and worship. Out of communication comes service and worship. You cannot worship if you do not know God. The more you know God, the more you know His heart, the more you know His purpose, the more you know what He has done, the more it gives you worship. Otherwise, worship is empty.

Oftentimes, I feel that when we are praising God or worshiping God, these are many words, beautiful words, but where is the substance? We do not know Him. We do not know His work and that is the reason why our worship is so weak. Worship is based on communion, on communication, and the more we know Him, the more it draws that worship from us. We find that He is worthy. We can place Him in the place where He ought to be; and also we realize what our place is. That is worship.

And, of course, service actually comes out of worship. Service leads back to worship, but service comes out of worship. If you try to serve but it does not come out of worship, it is not spiritual ministry. Spiritual ministry begins with God, and it has to come out of worship. If there is worship there cannot but be spiritual service. You cannot be just a worshiper and not a server. You cannot divide these two things. These two things go together. So, the meaning of the house is communication and worship with service.

David
A Place of Rest

Thirdly, after God gave David the kingdom and he dwelt in his palace, David said to Nathan: "I live in this house of cedar and yet the ark of God still lives in a tent. That is not right" So Nathan told him he could do whatever was in his heart. But immediately the word of God came to Nathan: "You go back and tell David…" (see I Chronicles 17:2 ff). If you go back and read I Chronicles 17, as you read it you will weep because when David had the desire to build a house for God, the whole idea is the idea of rest.

What is the house of God? The house of God is a place where God rests. Now David rested in his palace, and it was God who gave him rest. David lived a very restless life. He was a wanderer. He was a fugitive, he was hunted, he had to flee and hide in caves, he had many enemies, he had to fight many battles. He had a very restless life, but God, in His grace, gave David rest. Finally, you find God built David his house. He had his kingdom, his throne, his palace; he was rested. And when David was given rest, he became restless for God. Formerly, he was restless because of himself, but now he had gotten his rest; so he began to become restless for God. He was thinking of God's rest, and that very thought touched God's heart very deeply. God said to David through Nathan: "Since I have delivered the children of Israel out of Egypt I have wandered with them from tent to tent, from tabernacle to tabernacle, and even after I planted them in the land of promise, did I ever ask anyone to build me a house in which to live? I have not asked for it; yet you are the only one who wants to do it for Me."

It touched God's heart. Can we say that in the whole history of mankind from Adam and Eve after they sinned and were driven out of Eden, not only men became wanderers, but God lost His rest? Can a father rest if his sons or daughters are away as prodigals? There is no rest. God had no rest, and He is looking for a place of rest. He is looking to rest among mankind, but man did not give Him rest. Man gave Him lots of troubles. Only when Christ came into this world did God find His rest in Christ: "This is My beloved Son in whom I am well-pleased." But what God desires is not just one man; He wants a new mankind. He wants a new mankind that will give Him rest, that He can rest among His own people.

This is the meaning of the house of God—rest. But in a very real sense, we will never give God rest until He first gives us rest. That is very true. But when we are given His rest, there is a Sabbath, there is a rest prepared for us to enter (see Hebrews chapter 4). We need to enter into His rest. Why? because everything is done. Christ has done everything for us. On the cross He said, "It is finished." Everything is done. We can rest in Christ Jesus, and if we do rest in Christ Jesus, then it is time for us to get restless for God. Let us give God rest. He can rest when we really trust Him, when we really obey Him.

Our Lord Jesus learned obedience through the things which He suffered, and God finds rest in that Man. It is the same thing with us. God can only rest in us if we obey Him. Obedience is better than sacrifice. Just remember this.

Solomon
God's Name

Fourthly, eventually, Solomon built a house. Now when Solomon dedicated that temple, he said, "Will God indeed dwell in this house that I built?" (see II Chronicles 6). No, God is too great for that, but it is a place where God will put His name there. It is the place where people can come and pray because His eyes are upon that house, His ears are upon that house, and He will hear and forgive.

So what is the meaning of the house of God? The meaning of the house of God is where God puts His name. He puts His name in His house. "Where two or three are gathered together unto My name, there am I in the midst of them." That is the house of God. But unfortunately, when God put His name upon that temple, the children of Israel misrepresented that name completely. They disgraced that name, so eventually that temple had to be destroyed.

What about the church? The Lord said that He commits His name to the church. He commits Himself to the church. To put a name there is a commitment. When He commits Himself to the church, how do we react? Do we really honor that name? uphold that name? exalt that name? In other words, do we put ourselves under that name, under His authority, let Christ be the Head of the church, let Christ be the Lord of each of our lives? Do we honor His name? Or do we bring disgrace to His name? The name is given to the church, but whether it is under reproach or whether it is in praise depends on us.

The church is a place we can pray. You remember our Lord said, "Hereafter, I give you My name. You can pray to the Father in My name, and whatever you pray shall be done unto you" (see John 16). What does it mean when we use that name and pray? Does it mean that we pray in His name for our own interests? No, we pray in His name for His will to be done on earth as it is in heaven. So this is the meaning of the house of God.

Rebuilding the House of God
Love

Finally, you remember when the children of Israel came back from Babylonian captivity in the book of Ezra. They had lived in Babylon for seventy years. They had built their houses, they had built up their businesses, they lived a very comfortable life, and they were given much freedom even though they were slaves. They could worship God. They developed that ingenious religious system of synagogues that enabled them to worship God much more conveniently than the temple which had been destroyed.

Suddenly, they were free to go back to Jerusalem to rebuild the house of God. In other words, the only reason given to return to Jerusalem was to rebuild God's house, to restore God's name upon this earth that He may have a dwelling place. That was the only reason. Most of the Israelites remained in the land of captivity. They did not bother to go back. Why? If they returned they would return to a ruined city surrounded by enemies. They would be returning for only one reason and that was to build God's house. Now was God's house so important to their lives? Most people thought it was not that important: "Our houses are more important; our welfare is more important." So they stayed in the land of captivity—not ideal, but they stayed. Only a remnant, whose spirit was stirred, returned to build God's house totally out of love. There was no other reason—because they loved God, they loved His name. They were willing to forsake everything—their comforts, their businesses, their houses, their enterprises. They were willing to give up everything to go back to Jerusalem for God's sake to build a house for God that His name may be upon this earth. That is love.

What is the house of God? The house of God is a house of love. God is love, and if there is love, there is God's house.

In the seven letters to the churches (see Revelation 2-3), in the letter to the church in Ephesus, God said: "You have every good thing there, but you have left your first love. Repent. If you do not repent, I will remove your lampstand." Lampstand stands for the church in the sight of God. When that is removed it means the testimony is removed.

So what is the house of God? The house of God is a house of love. Only when we continue in our first love with Him is the house of God a reality. Whenever our love towards Him gets cold, repent. So remember, the house of God is not just a concept, something for us to speculate and talk about. The house of God is very real, and it ought to bring lots of conviction to us. It ought to bring us to our knees to repentance. It ought to bring us into renewed consecration and commitment to Him.

Finally, remember it is *God's* house. In other words, it has to satisfy Him. We are satisfied, but is He satisfied?

Dear heavenly Father, we do praise and thank Thee that Thou should so honor us as to even show us Thy heart, Thy desire, Thy longing. We do praise and thank Thee that Thou hast been so gracious to us in delivering us out of the world to bring us to Thyself that Thou mayest be able to build us into Thy house. And Thou wants to rest in us, to be loved, to be worshiped, to be honored, and to fellowship, to be in union. Oh, Lord, it is too much! We just cannot comprehend. We do ask Thee Lord, that Thou would continue to open our understanding and draw us into that reality and reveal to us how unfit we are.

Lord, give us a holy discontent that we may really repent and return to Thee. We want Thee to have that house. Oh, how we praise and thank Thee that one day Thou wilt have it. We know it; it is already there. We ask in Thy precious name. Amen.

The Building of the House

Matthew 16:18—And I also, I say unto thee that thou art Peter, and on this rock I will build my assembly, and hades' gates shall not prevail against it.

Hebrews 3:3-6—For he has been counted worthy of greater glory than Moses, by how much he that has built it has more honour than the house. For every house is built by some one; but he who has built all things [is] God. And Moses indeed [was] faithful in all his house, as a ministering servant, for a testimony of the things to be spoken after; but Christ, as Son over his house, whose house are we, if indeed we hold fast the boldness and the boast of hope firm to the end.

Hebrews 11:10,16—For he waited for the city which has foundations, of which God is [the] artificer and constructor... but now they seek a better, that is, a heavenly; wherefore God is not ashamed of them, to be called their God; for he has prepared for them a city.

I Corinthians 3:9-15—For we are God's fellow-workmen; ye are God's husbandry, God's building. According to the grace of God which has been given to me, as a wise architect, I have laid the foundation, but another builds upon it. But let each see how he builds upon it. For other foundation can no man lay besides that which [is] laid, which is Jesus Christ. Now if any one build upon [this] foundation, gold, silver, precious stones, wood, grass, straw, the work of each shall be made manifest; for the day shall declare [it], because it is revealed in fire; and the fire shall try the work of each what it is. If the work of any one which he has built upon [the foundation] shall abide, he shall receive a reward. If the work of any one shall be consumed, he shall suffer loss, but he shall be saved, but so as through [the] fire.

Ephesians 4:15-16—but, holding the truth in love, we may grow up to him in all things, who is the head, the Christ: from whom the whole body, fitted together, and connected by every joint of supply, according to [the] working in [its] measure of each one part, works for itself the increase of the body to its self-building up in love.

We have been considering before the Lord this matter of God's spiritual house. First of all, we mentioned that God had this very thing in His heart even before creation. He wanted a house, and that is why He created the universe. It is not in the sense that He created the universe to be His house because the heavens and the heaven of heavens cannot contain Him. The heavens are His throne, and the earth is His footstool, so what He created is not His house. God is not after a physical house. If He were after a physical house, He could easily create it for Himself. Therefore, we find that God created man because He is after a spiritual house. That spiritual house is made up of the man whom He created. He wanted to dwell among man. He wanted man to be His dwelling place, His home. And that is the eternal purpose of God.

In Hebrews 3:6 we are told: "… whose house are we, if indeed we hold fast the boldness and the boast of our confession firm to the end." In I Timothy 3:15 we are told that God's house is the church of the living God, the base and the pillar of truth. In a sense, we can see very clearly what this house or this home is that God is after from eternity to eternity. It is His church; we are His house if we hold fast the boldness and the boast of our confession to the end. So, it is of tremendous importance for us to understand what this house is. We are involved in it. We are to be that house and of course we want to know the meaning of this house.

We have shared together on two of the meanings of the house of God. We went through the Bible taking up some illustrations to illustrate the meaning of God's house. We will not go back and go over that again, but just mention it.

The house of God means the *union and communion of God and man in Christ Jesus*. Unworthy as we are, like Jacob; our God is holy and righteous. And yet it is His desire to come to us, it is His desire that we may be joined to Him and have communion with Him. How can it be done? It is through that ladder, our Lord Jesus. The first meaning of the house of God is the union and communion of God and man in Christ Jesus.

Then we find that God commanded Moses to build Him a tabernacle as His dwelling place. Why did He want that dwelling place? He wanted to communicate with His people. He wanted to speak to His people on the mercy seat between the two cherubim. Not only that, He also wanted us to speak to Him. He desires *fellowship*; He desires *communication*. Are we giving Him that?

In the heart of David, we find a desire to build a temple for God. It is *a place of rest*. Since man sinned, God has lost His rest. He has been seeking and looking for, and finding the lost man. He is longing to rest in man, but unless we first are rested in the finished work of Christ, we will not be able to give Him that rest.

Then we find Solomon built a temple, not because he believed that God would really dwell in that temple, but he believed that *God would put His name there*. God would commit Himself there and listen to the prayers of the people who prayed in that house or prayed toward that house. What is the church? "Where two or three are gathered together unto My name, there am I in the midst of them" (see Matthew 18:20). Our Lord Jesus has committed His name to the church and because of this, how much we need to be committed to that name.

Finally, we mentioned that the remnant returned to rebuild the temple and they did it out of pure love. So, what is the church? The *church is a house of love*. These are the things we have covered.

Now we would like to consider together before the Lord this matter of the building of God's house. It is really eye-opening when you read the Scripture. You find that whenever the house is mentioned, the word "build" is used. Or to put it another way, the house is to be built, it is not to be created. Our God is the God of creation, but He is also a great builder. By His wisdom and power He *created* the heavens and the earth, but He *built* His church by giving His own Son. The building of the house is a greater work than the creation of the universe. In creating the universe, God only used His wisdom and His power; He is not, in a sense, directly involved. But in building His house, He is so involved Himself that He even gave up His own beloved Son. The cost is so much greater because the house is so much nearer and dearer to His heart. We admire His creation, but do we admire His house? We love His creation; we enjoy His creation, but how much do we really love His house? He gave everything for that house in giving up His own Son. If this is the case, do you think we can give more for that house? Do you think that in giving to that house it will be too much? If it cost God everything, if you love the house of God, it should cost you all.

In types, this matter of the building of God's house is found throughout the Scripture. Even from the very beginning, in Genesis chapter 1, you find that God created man in His own image after His likeness, male and female created He them.

That is the creation of man, but when you come into the actual work of creating man in chapter 2, there, God took the dust, the red earth and formed it into a body. He breathed into that body's nostril the breath of life. And the Bible says man became a living soul. Thus, Adam was created.

Then God said, "It is not good for man to be alone." So you find that God led all the living creatures that He had created one by one to Adam. I personally feel it is the law of elimination because God said that it was not good for man to be alone. He needs a helpmeet, a counterpart, his like. So God brought all these living creatures to him, the big, the small, the strange; all kinds of animals were brought to Adam for him to look at them. It was more than just a task of asking Adam to name these animals. Of course, he named all of them, every one of them—he was a natural zoologist. He did not need to go to school. By naming them he put them in their specific area, but he could not find his like in any of these animals. So God put him to sleep and took one of his ribs out of his side. (In the original it says, "God took something out of him." We do not know if it was a rib or not.) However, God took something out of him and built a woman. Man was created, but woman was built; she was built out of man. God did not take another lump of clay and form the female from it and breathe into it so that she became a living woman. God did not do that. He took something out of Adam and built that something into a woman.

Then God woke Adam and led that woman to Adam just like He led all the other animals to Adam. But when the woman was led to Adam, he looked at her and said: "I see myself in her. This is me—part of me, bone of my bones, flesh of my flesh. Call her a woman." And the two became one flesh.

What is Building?

We know that Adam and Eve are types of Christ and the church. What is the meaning of building? We know in studying the Bible there is a principle called the principle of first mentioning. Whenever something is mentioned the first time in the Scripture, it usually gives you the basic idea of what that is. According to the principle of first mentioning that word "build" is used the first time in the Bible in the building of the woman. What is the basic meaning of building? Building is different from creating because creating is producing something out of nothing. There was nothing there—no material, nothing—and God just used His word. He spoke a word and it was done. In other words, He created the whole universe out of nothing. That is creation.

Building is different. Building is taking something out of the original creation and building it up into something. That is the basic idea of building. Apply it to Christ and the church. God said, "It is not good for Him to be alone." Even before the foundation of the world, in eternity past, if we may say, there was only God the Father, God the Son, God the Spirit—the triune God. They were self-existing and one. One day, in eternity past, the Father looked at the Son. He loved His Son so much, He said, "It is not good for My Son to be alone. I will give Him a helpmeet, His like." God had that idea even before He started creating the universe, and that is the reason why He created man. But unfortunately, that man fell into sin, and since that time, God was looking for that one who could be His Son's helpmeet, His Son's counterpart, just like His Son. But He could not find it. Finally, He had to send His Son into this world.

Do you know why our Lord Jesus came into this world? The Gospel of John is the Gospel that gives us the inner meaning of the life of Christ. Why did God's Son come into this world? According to the other Gospels, you find He came into this world to seek and to save the lost, but if you read the Gospel according to John you get into the inner meaning or you get into the very mind of God. You find that God sent His Son into this world for one purpose: to seek for His bride, to look for His counterpart. He was on earth for thirty-three years, and He looked everywhere but He could not find His like, His counterpart. So finally, God put Him to sleep. But His sleep was different from Adam's sleep because when God put Adam to sleep there was no sin in the world yet. Sin had not come into the world yet. So you find that Adam's sleep was a very peaceful sleep. And not only that, that operation was a painless operation; there was no blood. But with our Lord Jesus it was different. Man had sinned dreadfully; so the Son of God, the Son of Man had to bear our sins in His body. He who knew no sin was made sin for us. It is a mystery. We do not understand. We could understand somewhat our Lord's rejection by man. We could understand somewhat the attack of the enemy, of Satan, when our Lord was upon the cross.

In other words, we could understand the first three hours of our Lord's crucifixion because during the first three hours, He suffered from the hand of man and the powers of darkness. We could understand a little bit of that, but we cannot understand the last three hours. At mid-day the sun hid its face and the earth turned into darkness. Why? Because God made Him sin for us. All our sins came upon this pure and spotless Lamb of God. He was made sin and because He was made sin, God, the righteous One, crushed Him and departed from Him. So our Lord cried out, "My God, My God." He did not say, "My Father, My Father." He had such sweet fellowship with His Father through eternity and when He was on earth there was uninterrupted communion. He always pleased the Father. He did the things the Father wanted Him to do. The Father was always with Him. He always saw the Father's smiling face, but during that time He could only say, "My God, My God." Why? He stood in our ground, a corrupted, defiled, sinful, rebellious old creation. "My God, My God, why hast Thou forsaken Me?" It was a painful death; but thank God, before He gave up His spirit, He said, "It is finished." The work is done. He has borne our sins in His body on the tree.

The next day was a Sabbath day, and the Jews honored that day and would not allow anybody to be hung there because to be hung on the cross is a curse. So the soldiers came and broke the legs of the two robbers to speed up their death because they were strong and still living. But when they came to our Lord Jesus, they saw that He was already dead. To make sure that He was dead, a soldier thrust a spear through His side and out from His side came blood and water (see John 19). John was there. He saw the spear thrust in, and he saw it drawn out; He saw the blood and the water, and he bore testimony that what he saw was true that you may believe.

Now why did John make it so emphatic? What is the meaning of that? It is because there you find God put our Lord Jesus to sleep, to death, and out of Him God took something—blood and water. I do not know, but some people say that was the last drop of blood still in His heart. He shed all His blood and there was still some remaining in His heart, but He died of a broken heart, so the blood disintegrated into blood and water. Something was taken out of His side, from His very heart— blood to atone our sins, water to give us life.

Out of the body of our Lord Jesus, God took blood and water and with this blood and water He built the church. So brothers and sisters, if we remember this: blood to atone for our sins, water to give us life. It is only when our sins are atoned, and we have His own life in us—this is the material that He builds the church. It is coming out of Him; therefore He can say, "This is Me."

What is the church? The church is Christ in His corporate expression. The church is the extension of Christ. He looks at the church and says, "This is Me, My flesh, My bone." And because of this the church can be united with Him in one spirit. He builds the church.

We have mentioned Jacob. Jacob thought that if God would bless him, give him food to eat, garments to wear, and lead him safely, peacefully back home, then he would make God his God, and he would use the pillar that he had used for his pillow. He set it up and said, "This pillar shall be the house of God and I will give one-tenth to Him" (see Genesis 28:22). Jacob thought that if God should bless him then he would serve God, he would build God a house. Actually he built God a monument, not a house, because a pillar is a monument; it is not a house. He would build God a monument and also he would give God one-tenth. In other words, to show his gratitude he would serve God with his work, with his service. He thought that was the way to build the house of God. But God said, "No." God would take hold of

Jacob, this original person, and transform him into Israel, and with Israel he would build His house.

The same thing is true with the children of Israel. God redeemed them out of Egypt, and not only were they redeemed, but their women, their children, their cattle, and their sheep were all taken out of Egypt. But more than that, before they left Egypt they spoiled Egypt of her wealth (see Exodus 12:36). Egypt was a very wealthy nation at that time and when they came out, they literally spoiled Egypt of her wealth. They had gold and silver and all these precious things with them. They became not only a free people but a wealthy people. Now how are they going to live their lives? How are they going to use their wealth? They could have easily lived a very comfortable life, a luxurious life, enjoying themselves because they had the wealth. But God asked them for a heave-offering, which is a love offering. They were to offer what God had given them to build that tabernacle.

You know, it is very easy for God to drop a tabernacle from heaven. In the book of Acts, when Peter was on that roof at noontime, he must have been hungry; so he was thinking of food when he was praying. And God gave him a vision of a white sheet coming down from heaven full of quadrupeds and creeping things. And the voice said, "Rise, kill and eat." Now surely, God could also easily drop a tabernacle from heaven and say, "Now I am going to dwell among you." No, for

God to do that would be creation, not building. So God said to offer a heave-offering. Out of what He had redeemed, they were to give and with that build the tabernacle. That is building.

So you see the basic idea of the building of the church is: You take something that God has already given, and then you build it into the house of God. That is the concept.

Who is the Builder?

The Lord Jesus said, "I will build My church upon this rock and the gates of Hades shall not prevail against it." The church is so precious to our Lord, He cannot commit the building of it to anyone other than Himself. So He said, "I will build My church upon this rock." He is the builder, the only builder, the only One who can build God's house. Many people can build, but He is the only One who can build a house for God to rest. He is the only One who is able to do that, nobody else. You cannot do that, I cannot do that, none of us can do that, the angels cannot do that. Only our Lord Jesus can build His church.

In Hebrews 3:3-6, it is said that Christ should have more honor than Moses, just as the builder of the house is more honorable than the house. So here you find Moses is the house and the Lord is the One who builds Moses. And in Hebrews chapter 11 you find Abraham, Isaac, and Jacob wandered in the Promised Land as sojourners. If they wanted to go back to their homeland, Ur of Chaldea, they could do that, or even halfway to Haran, they could do that. But they were looking for a city with foundations, whose architect and constructor is God. God has prepared for us a better city. This is the city that you find in Revelation chapters 21 and 22. That is God's house, God and man dwelling together in unity for eternity.

Now who is able to build that house except God Himself? God cannot trust anyone to be the architect of that house. No architect has the wisdom to draw the design. He cannot trust anyone to construct it. No construction company in the world can do this job. God alone is the builder. Brothers and sisters, we cannot emphasize this enough because we find in Christianity today, out of good intentions, we are trying to build God's house. We have been trying for almost two thousand years, and what do we get? We get the tower of Babel, not the house of God. Therefore I hope there is none among us who has a secret desire to build the house of God. You better give that up. Today we hear about lots of church planters, church builders, but what they build is the tower of Babel to spread their names, not to give God rest. We cannot build it; do not try. God is the only builder. HE designs it. HE builds it. HE does everything in it.

You may challenge me and say, "In the very beginning, didn't you read some scriptures that tell us we are the builders?" Paul said in I Corinthians chapter 3, "We are God's workmen, and you are

God's husbandry and God's building. I am like a wise master builder." Some versions say, "a wise architect," and some versions say, "an expert builder, a master builder." But as a matter of fact, if you try to put it more properly, probably what Paul means is, "I am a wise, chief foreman." So here Paul said, "I am a master builder. I lay the foundation, even Christ Jesus, and there can be no other foundation but Christ;" and then "each one of you." Remember, he wrote to the Corinthian believers and to all who call upon the name of the Lord, so we are included. You—each one of you—pay attention to what you build upon it. If you build with gold, silver, and precious stones, or you build with wood, straw, and stubble, one day fire will appear and test what you build. If you build with gold, silver, and precious stone, it will just glorify it and you will receive a reward. But if you build with wood, straw, and hay, it will be burned, but you will be saved, barely saved. So you are building. Every day you are building. Every day you are building something up.

Then in Ephesians chapter 4, you find that all the different members of the body work together, fit together, according to the measure that God has given to each for the self-building up in love. In other words, we are all involved in this building work. No one is excluded unless you are not the Lord's. If you are the Lord's, you are involved in that building. How are you going to reconcile these two opposites?

I think there is one verse that can solve this problem and it is found in Philippians chapter 2:

> So that, my beloved, even as ye have always obeyed, not as in my presence only, but now much rather in my absence, work out your own salvation with fear and trembling, for it is God who works in you both the willing and the working according to his good pleasure (vv. 12-13).

Indeed, the Lord Himself is the only builder, but how does He build? He first works in you that you may work out with fear and trembling. Do you see this picture? In other words, it is not that you have an idea of what the house of God should be like, so you draw up a blueprint. As if you are the architect; you give it the concept. No. God is the architect. He is the One who has that concept of the house of God. He is the One who draws the blueprint, but He works this in you by revelation. He reveals that to you and after you receive that revelation and understand it, it is working out of you. So who is working? Who is building? He builds. He builds in you, through you. After all the work is done, all you can say is: He has done it. You have not done anything because all that comes out of you is what He has worked in you.

The same thing is true not only with the blueprint, it is true with the whole process of building. You find that everything that is put into the house of God He first works in you, and then works out from you with fear and trembling. All the materials He first works in you, then you give it back to Him with fear and trembling. He first gives you all the power, then He works it out from you. Thank God, He wants us to work together with Him, but actually He does all the work, and we share the glory.

I always remember the story of a father who was going to move a table. It was a heavy one, but the father was strong. He began to lift up the table and his little boy said, "Father, let me help you." The father said, "Good, I need your help." So he allowed that boy to hold one of the legs and together they moved the table. As a matter of fact, the boy put more weight on that table. So the father bears not only the table but also the boy. Finally, he moved the table and the boy said, "Father, we have done it!" Now that is what it is.

How He loves us and honors us. And that is the reason why after everything is done you have to go back and say, "We are but unprofitable servants." He is the builder. If only we can remember this, it will save us lots of headaches, and not only us but also our brothers and sisters.

How Does God Build?

We need to go into some of the building processes. It is important because that is how the house is built. God created man with the idea of building man into His house. But unfortunately, man did not obey God. Man did not follow God. Man did not eat the tree of life. If man should eat the tree of life they would receive that uncreated, divine life in them and thus they could be united with God in life. And from that life it can be developed into the house. But unfortunately, man ate the tree of the knowledge of good and evil. Man declared independence of God. Man fell into himself. Man became flesh. His spirit died, and he lost contact with God. Mankind became slaves to sin, to the enemy, under the bondage of death. Satan holds that bondage over man. So when God looked at this material, could He take it up and build His house? That clay was marred before it became a vessel. There was no way to repair it. We are always thinking of trying to repair it, to reform it, to beautify it, to decorate it, to add something to it, and then it will become something for God. No. God looked at man and said what can I do with it? I cannot do anything with it. I cannot build My house with this kind of polluted, defiled material. The Holy God cannot dwell in that unclean house. No, He could not.

The Work of Redemption

So the first thing God had to do was to send His beloved Son into this world to do the work of redemption. God did not throw man away completely and say, "Well, this is finished; I will create another kind of man, maybe one without a free

124

will. Then, I can build them to be My house." God is *the* free will. How could God, the free will, dwell in a creation with no free will? He could not do that. It is not like Him. There is no counterpart. And yet you find God did something marvelous. I do not remember who said this, maybe Moody: "God will take what the devil casts away and say, 'I will have it.'" And that is what it is. We are a bunch of nothing, worse than nothing, and God had to do a tremendous work. Every time you think of redemption, you see the heart of God. He should throw us away, but He could not. He loved us. So He had to give us His Son. Jesus had to die for us in order that He may give us a new life. "If anyone be in Christ, he is a new creation; the old things have passed away; all things are made new and all things are of God" (see II Corinthians 5:17).

You do not know the cost that God paid in building His house. The first thing is that He has to do a work of redemption. He has to bring in a new mankind, a new race, a new creation, a people whose sins are forgiven, who are righteous in the sight of God, a people who now have His own life. That is the first thing God has to do.

Living Stones

The building material of God is man[1], but not just any kind of man, not just a man that we know. God builds with man, but it is a new man, a born-from-above man, a regenerated man, a man with God's life in him. That life in him—that new creation—is the building material. You are not the building material; I am not the building material. It is the new creation in you; it is Christ in you. It is life in you that is the building material. That is the reason why you find when Peter confessed Jesus as the Christ, the Son of the living God, He said to Peter: "You are Peter, you are a stone. Formerly, you were dust, earth, clay, but now, on your confession, a new element has entered into your life. You now become a living stone." So as we come to the Lord, first, we are turned from dust into stone. How is the tower of Babel built? It is built with brick, and brick is mixing earth with straw. But the house of God is built with stones— living stones— the life of God in them. That is the building block.

What is the church? We say the church is the gathering of the believers, the gathering of you and me. That is just the problem of the church. The problem of the church is because of you and me. We come in and try to build with wood, hay,

---

[1] The term *man* here is inclusive of men and women, as in *mankind*.

straw, and stubble. Instead of letting Christ's life in us be the building material, we come in with our human nature, our own glory, our own energy, our own work, and we say we are building the church. That is the tower of Babel we are building. We have to build with gold, silver, and precious stones. It is the Christ in you, it is the Christ in me, the hope of glory. You have no hope of glory. I have no hope of glory. The hope of glory is Christ in you and me.

So what is the church? The church is Christ in His corporate expression. The Christ in you, the Christ in me is built together. These living stones are built together and that builds the church. So anything that is you, anything that is me, has to be separated by the cross before we enter into the church. Wherever we try to bring anything of ourselves into the church, remember we destroy the church, we do not build the church. The church is an awesome thing. We need to build it with fear and trembling.

Precious Stones

Not only that, we find that when the Lord builds with stones, these are not just stones, these are precious stones. In the holy city, the new Jerusalem, you find precious stones—not just stones. Sometimes we think that as long as we are saved, God just builds all the saved ones together into His house. But what you build is a nursery—all babies.

There is weeping here, crying there, and every baby is very self-centered. At midnight, if babies are not happy they cry. If you do not cater to their desires quick enough they get angry. And that is what you have today. God builds not just stones, not just babes in Christ; God builds with precious stones.

How can stones be turned into precious stones? Precious stones are a compound, not an element. You find all these different elements buried deep down in the earth in darkness for centuries under great pressure and heat. Eventually, certain elements begin to be compounded together to become a precious stone, and this precious stone is different from the other precious stone. Brothers and sisters, God builds with precious stones only. Our Lord is a precious stone Himself. He is not just a living stone but a precious stone. What is that? That is character. To simply have life is not enough; this life has to develop, to grow into character. When life follows its nature it becomes character. Every life has a nature, but if you follow that nature long enough it becomes a character. If you do not follow that nature, it does not become a character. It still remains in that immature stage. We have too many babies in the church. On the one hand, it is good because we love babies. But on the other hand, it breaks our Father's heart because we are always in the self-centered stage of receiving, receiving, receiving. Everything is for me. God is for me. Christ is for me. Everybody is for me, me, me. How can you build the church, God's house?

Character building is painful. That is the reason why I always feel that if God saved me He should rapture me to Him right away. That would save me all kinds of temptations, all kinds of trials. Why does He leave me on this earth, miserable earth, passing through all these trials and testings and many failures? Why? It is because He wants us to be precious stones. He wants to develop character in us through sufferings, through pressure, through darkness, through heat that we may find the different elements of His divine life begin to form in a special way, and become character. Peter is one precious stone; John is another precious stone, but they each manifest Christ. It is not Peter, not John, and yet it is divine character in Peter, and divine character in John. All the character of Christ must be developed within us through much suffering. Suffering is good.

Stones Fitted Together

However, it is not just precious stones. If you go to a museum, you see some precious stones displayed there for people to look at and admire. Some people hope they may have it, but that is not God's purpose. God's purpose is not just to create some spiritual giants that He can display to the world. What is the use of that? It only brings spiritual pride to you. God is too practical for that. In one sense it is important to see these stones being developed into precious stones. Every one is a precious stone with different combinations of the nature of Christ in a special way. Only you have it in a special way and another brother or sister has it in another special way. There is an individuality that God loves. Even in eternity there is an individuality there. Peter is always Peter, even though he is a different Peter than when he was a rough stone. He becomes a precious stone, but it is still Peter. There is an individuality there. It is precious, brothers and sisters. You are you and God wants you to be what He wants you to be. He does not want you to be somebody else. He is developing you in an individual way. He loves it, and I hope you love it too.

Individuality is something that will continue to eternity, but individualism must be dealt with. In other words, you are still one precious stone, but that one precious stone has to be fitted together and joined together with other precious stones. You cannot maintain your individualism and say, "No, I am going to stand here alone to be an example of the wonderful work of God." That is not God's purpose for you. It is not for your glory; it is for His glory. So you find that these stones have to be fitted together, and that is the problem. The more precious that stone becomes, the more difficult for it to be fitted with another.

When you quarry [extract] these precious stones out of the mine, you have to do a lot of work on these stones. When you take them out of the mine, you do not see any radiance, any luster, any light there. It is covered with dirt, and you need to do lots of breaking, cutting, and purifying work to take off all the dross that are attached to those precious stones.

This is the same thing with us. Even though the Lord is working within each one of us to develop us as precious stones, we still carry with us a big load of all kinds of things, right? We still have the world upon us; maybe we still have some sin; we still have some weight upon us. We still have our flesh there. We still have the self there. Brothers and sisters, all these things need to be purified. That is the reason why we find in Ephesians chapter 5 the Lord loved His church and gave Himself for her. He sanctifies her, purifying her by the water of the word that she may become a glorious church without spot or wrinkle or any of such sort. Dear brothers and sisters, the cross has to work in our lives to purify us from all the dross that we carry with us.

Do you not find sometimes that there is just too much dross in you? Do you accept the working of the cross in your life? The cross is not only a subjective truth—that is the foundation—but on that foundation we must allow the Holy Spirit to apply that cross to our daily life. He will enlighten us. He will show us where the dross is. He will show us where it needs to be purified. His word will divide the soul and the spirit. It will penetrate, kill, divide it, and let us see that this is soul, not the spirit. It has to be purified. Our flesh has to be brought to death. Our "self" must be denied. These works of the cross have to be going on in your life in order that you may be fitted together with one another.

Cutting

More than that, even though all this dross is purified, you still cannot fit with one another. You need to be cut, sawed, chiseled, smoothed, according to your brother and sister that will be built to your right, to your left, below, and above, according to God's wisdom. Here is a big piece of precious stone, but to fit in with another precious stone, even some part of that precious stone has to be cut off to be made into the house.

Some brothers and sisters are too great to be cut. They are too big to be built with other brothers and sisters. They want everybody to be cut so they can occupy a place larger than God's design. Even the gift that God has given to you needs to be dealt with. Do not think because this is given by God it is spiritual gift. Look at the Corinthian church. Even this gift has to be regulated that everything will be orderly and done in comeliness. Think of that! It is not because God has given you this gift therefore everywhere you go you say, "My gift." Sometimes your gift has to be hidden for a while, laid aside for a while. It is not the time to use it according to the proportion of faith.

What is wrong with our spirituality? Oftentimes, our spirituality frightens our brothers and sisters away. We want to measure everyone with our spirituality; therefore when we meet a brother or sister, all they get is condemnation. We judge them. It shows that we need to be cut. Sometimes God may even take away our spiritual virtues. God has to break us down to make us pliable in His hand that we may be fitted together with our brothers and sisters.

We are told that when the temple was built all the stones that were quarried out of the mine actually were discovered under Mount Moriah. The masons would go into these mines and cut the stones according to the pattern. There is a plan there. Every stone in the temple is already planned and every stone is numbered, and all these stones were cut in the mine in darkness. So when they were transported up to Mount Moriah to be put together, there was not a sound of hammer or the sound of iron (see I Kings 6:7). All these stones were put together quietly without making any noise. There was no need for any further iron work, so there was no spark or fire. They were just put one to another and they fit so beautifully because everyone was cut according to measure, according to one another.

Many times, God's dealings with us are more than just personal. Personally, you may not need these dealings, but because God wants to fit you with the brothers and sisters, therefore, you have to go through all these dealings. A shoulder must be cut, a corner must be cut; something smooth must be chiseled and even sawed through. So brothers and sisters, God has a place for you in His house. It is already labeled. You are number so-and-so, and you will be put in a certain position—only you, nobody else—and you will have another number next to you. God has already put the number there and according to that He is sawing you, cutting you, chiseling you, and smoothing you. How patient the Holy Spirit is, but how impatient we are.

All these works have to be done in darkness, in hidden places, in your private closet. If this work is not done, you will find that when all these stones are put together, you have to hear the sound of hammer and iron, lots of sparks. And that is what you are having now because you have not allowed the Holy Spirit to complete His work in your life.

We need one another. I cannot do without you; you cannot do without me. The Lord cannot do without any one of us. And that is the house. It is an awesome thing, a dreadful place, but it is the gate of heaven (see Genesis 28:17).

What I am trying to say is simply this: the building of God's house is not a common thing. It is most precious in God's heart, and hopefully, it becomes very precious to our heart. God spent everything for that house. Are we willing to spend all that God has given us? Actually, we have nothing; it is all given. But are we willing to put our all in

His hands and let Him do whatever is necessary to make us fit to be put into the place He has ordained for each one of us?

In Revelation chapters 21 and 22 we find that house appears, that holy city, the New Jerusalem, a glorious church without spot or wrinkle or any such sort, a bride suitable to the Bridegroom in union forever, ruling and reigning in glory. Brothers and sisters, this is the purpose of God with you and with me. May the Lord have mercy upon us.

Dear heavenly Father, we acknowledge that human words are so inadequate. Even our understanding is so limited. We are not able really to enter into Thy heart, Thy mind, Thy love. We really are not able to feel how Thou feels concerning the house, that rest that Thou art seeking for. But Lord, we do pray that in Thy mercy and grace, Thou wilt at least give us a glimpse of it. We pray that Thou wilt touch our hearts. Give us at least a heart for Thy house.

Lord, we do acknowledge that when we see what Thy house really is, to us it is dreadful—dreadful to our flesh—but Lord, we want to commit ourselves to Thee for that house. Do whatever is necessary in each one of us. Do not let us go. Remember, tonight, we have committed ourselves to Thee and to Thy house. Thou art faithful. Perfect Thy work, Thy praise, and Thy glory. We ask in the name of our Lord Jesus. Amen.

Questions About the Spiritual House

Question #1 – You say that in John's Gospel Christ's coming to earth was to seek a bride. Could you please share with us a verse or text where this is stated or indicated?

> He that has the bride is the bridegroom; but the friend of the bridegroom, who stands and hears him, rejoices in heart because of the voice of the bridegroom: this my joy then is fulfilled. He must increase, but I must decrease (John 3:29-30).

Here you find the declaration made by John the Baptist, the forerunner of our Lord Jesus. We usually remember that John declared the Lord as the Lamb of God and He is. Some may even remember that John declared that our Lord is the Baptizer with the Holy Spirit and that is true. But probably, many do not remember that John also testified that our Lord Jesus is the Bridegroom. So when they questioned him about his ministry and his relationship, he said: "I am the friend of the bridegroom and when I hear the voice of the bridegroom, I rejoice. I must decrease but He must increase."

So here is a very clear testimony telling us that our Lord Jesus is the Bridegroom and He came into the world to seek for His bride. We know that

John's Gospel is different from the other three synoptic Gospels because they give us, more or less, the outward story of our Lord Jesus, but John is used of the Lord to give us the inward story of our Lord Jesus. So outwardly, He came into this world to seek and to save the lost, but John shows us why He came to seek and to save the lost. In other words, He did not come just to seek and save the lost that people will be saved and go to heaven. It is more than that. He came to seek and to save the lost because He was looking for His bride. He could not find His bride anywhere, so in a sense He had to bring people into the place where they can become His bride. That is why you find in John's Gospel the Lord talking to Nicodemus, the Lord talking to the Samaritan woman, the Lord doing different things there. All these things are signs. In other words, all the wonders our Lord did are not just wonders, but all these wonders have something behind them. They point to something. The Lord is gathering a people, giving them life, transforming them and bringing them together so that this people eventually will become His bride. And that is the inner reason for the coming of the Lord to this earth.

Remember, in the Gospel of John, how He brought in this one and that one and then, in chapter 13, He began to gather more with the eleven? In other words, it is more than just trying to bring this one in and that one in, but those whom He brought in, He was trying to build them together, put them together. And then, you will also remember that on that day, when the Spirit is given, they will be in Him, He will be in them, and they all will be one. So, the whole Gospel of John has that in view. Our Lord Jesus is the Bridegroom seeking for His bride and He has to make us suitable to be His bride. That is the reason I personally feel that the Gospel of John has a different emphasis to it.

Question #2 – You mentioned that we personally might not need to be cut but for the sake of being fitted with the others. Do you mean then, that there are those who have to be cut more than the others because of His sovereign choice? If this is the case, will there be more rewards in eternity?

First of all, if I said that some do not need to be cut personally, then I have said it wrong—I hope I have not said that. In other words, personally, all of us need to be cut. There is so much in every one of us that needs to be purified, needs to be cast away, needs to be cut. There is no exception.

Number two, there is also no exception for every one of us to be cut corporately. Not only do we need God's dealings individually so that each may become a precious stone, but corporately, all the precious stones, not one exception, need to be cut in order to be fitted together. So do not think that you can be an exception. It is a privilege and an honor that we all share. It is true that some may have to be cut more because there is too much of self, but all of us need to be cut in order to be fitted to one another.

I think probably I did not make it very clear. I mentioned that our gifts, not only what is natural, but even what is spiritual, our spiritual gifts need to be cut and purified. What the Lord has really worked in us, given to us—gifts, virtues, experiences of Himself, knowledge of Himself, those that really came from Him and are constituted, incorporated, built, worked in us—even these need to be cut and dealt with.

If what is given by God needs to be cut, does it mean that God has given us gifts of virtues, of experience, of knowledge of Himself, and these will be thrown away as waste? I do not think so. I think that what God has given to us is meant to be there for His glory. But what do we mean that these things need to be cut? Number one, it means that we all need to be balanced; so the cutting actually means to be balanced. God will give you some spiritual character which is wonderful and beautiful. It is Christ, it is your spiritual strength, but you may be lacking in some other aspect of the character of Christ. You need your brothers and sisters to balance you. Otherwise, you will be strong in one direction, and it will become a kind of sharp corner. This will not only touch others, but it will even hurt others.

Now suppose you are very strong in this matter of righteousness. Not only do you know the righteousness of Christ that God has made to you, but you have developed a practical righteousness, the righteousness of the saints. Suppose you develop very strongly in that direction. That is good, but because you are so righteous in all things, naturally that gives you a kind of discernment whenever you see something unrighteous. Immediately, you notice it because God has dealt very strongly with you on that point. Whenever you see any brothers or sisters doing something, saying something, or acting in ways that are not righteous according to the light God has given you and the experience you have, you are very tempted to judge your brothers and sisters. Therefore, you need some brothers and sisters who know the love of God or the mercies of God and have learned it in their life experience to a great degree to balance you. That is what I mean by cutting. In other words, you are not just going in one direction, but there are other brothers and sisters who will balance you so that you will be in the right position.

How we need the balance of our brothers and sisters! That is cutting, in a sense, because you feel that you are being restricted, you cannot go all the way with all your brothers and sisters, that they all must know the righteousness of God as you do. Sometimes you have to be more tolerant with your brothers and sisters and you have to see that you need the kindness and the love of God in you to balance up with your righteousness. This is cutting. So even our spiritual quality that God has given to us needs to be balanced. It must be put in the right position so it will not be just like a corner that sticks out.

Another meaning is that even our spiritual gifts and virtues need to be cut. If there are those who have the gift of tongues and all want to exercise their gifts, it will cause confusion because everybody is exercising his gift. Even with prophecy, it is the same thing. That is the reason why we need to see the "two or three" (see I Corinthians 14:26-29). There will be a divine order, and if you are prophesying and a brother there receives a revelation, then you cannot say, "Well, let me finish my prophesying." The Lord said for you to stop and let the brother with the revelation share what the Lord has revealed to him—now that is cutting. Oftentimes we think, "Because I have the gift, I must exercise my gift no matter what. I do not care about other people. This is my gift and I have to use it." It is true, you should use your gift. But in the house of God there is an order, and everything must be done comely, beautifully, so that there will be no confusion.

The same thing is true about grace or virtues or character that God has built in us. We find this in Ephesians 4:1-3:

> I, the prisoner in the Lord, exhort you therefore to walk worthy of the calling wherewith ye have been called, with all lowliness and meekness, with longsuffering, bearing with one another in

love; using diligence to keep the unity of the
Spirit in the uniting bond of peace.

How are we going to fulfill our calling to be the
body of Christ? We need lowliness and meekness
with long-suffering, bearing with one another in
love. We need lowliness. That is the way to fulfill
the calling. When God gives us spiritual gifts and
virtues, unfortunately, our flesh will glory in these
things instead of these things humbling us. That is
not why God gives us these gifts and virtues. We
need lowliness and meekness.

To put it another way, if you have spirituality,
or these spiritual things, you may have spiritual
pride. Of course, there is no such thing as pride being spiritual. We call it spiritual pride because you
are proud of your spirituality and, because of your
spirituality, you lose that lowliness, that meekness.
You cannot bear with other people. You cannot
suffer long. If you are put with a group of babies,
you get impatient. You want them to grow as
quickly as you do. You pull them up. But when
God puts you into the house of God, there are babies, children, and young people. Now you are fathers, and being fathers, you have to exercise all
lowliness and meekness with long-suffering, bearing with one another. And that is what I meant by
cutting off. In other words, you cannot go all the
way that you want to. You have to think of your
brothers and sisters and try to lower yourself to
their level to understand them, to love them, to fel-

lowship with them and gradually to bring them up. This is what is needed today; it is much needed today. And this is what I meant by being cut. You will find that in Philippians 2:1-4:

> If then there be any comfort in Christ, if any consolation of love, if any fellowship of the Spirit, if any bowels and compassions, fulfill my joy, that ye may think the same thing, having the same love, joined in soul, thinking one thing; let nothing be in the spirit of strife or vain glory, but, in lowliness of mind, each esteeming the other as more excellent than themselves; regarding not each his own qualities, but each those of others also (Philippians 2:1-4).

When you have spiritual gifts and virtues, you are in a position to comfort people, you are in a position to console people, you are in a position to fellowship, to share Christ with people. But in order to do that you need to have the spirit of lowliness of mind, esteeming others as more excellent than yourself. In other words, you need the mind of Christ. The mind of Christ is the mind of humility. With all that God has given you, you need the mind of Christ in order to be a comfort in Christ to other people, in order to console people in love, in order to pour out your compassion. Otherwise, the more spiritual you are, the less you are able to comfort people. You are more able to condemn people, less able to comfort people. When you are fellowshiping with brothers and sisters, your spirituality needs to be cut, but not in a sense that you become less lovely or less righteous. I do not mean that. It simply means that you have to lower yourself to the level of your brothers and sisters in order that you can fellowship and minister to them.

Look at Christ. He is full of virtues, fullness, and yet, He could fellowship with His disciples. It must have been such a restraint on His part, such a limitation on His part. Often He tried to convey Himself, but His disciples did not understand. Even so, the Lord did not say, "Well, you are off—helpless." Our Lord Jesus continued to love them, to wash their feet, trying to bring them up. Now, in a sense, you find the limitation that our Lord Jesus must have suffered throughout His life with His disciples. Now that is what we mean by cutting. So, what God has given to you is never lost. It will be there in eternity, but it needs to be disciplined. That is actually what we mean.

Part Three:
Spiritual Submission

What is Spiritual Submission?

Ephesians 5:21—Submitting yourselves to one another in the fear of Christ.

I Samuel 15:22-23a—Has Jehovah delight in burnt-offerings and sacrifices, as in hearkening to the voice of Jehovah? Behold, obedience is better than sacrifice, attention than the fat of rams. For rebellion is as the sin of divination, and selfwill is as iniquity and idolatry.

Dear heavenly Father, we do praise and thank Thee for Thy gracious provision, for the blood of Thy beloved Son, and the new and living way that He has dedicated for us. And with Him as our great High Priest we dare to approach Thy throne of grace. We thank Thee that we are now in Thy presence. May Thy glory fill the house. Lord, we ask that everything that stands against Thee will be removed at this moment. We pray that we may be before Thee, laid bare under Thy light. Let us see light in Thy light. We trust Thy Holy Spirit to open our eyes and understanding that we may truly be led into Thy truth. We acknowledge, Lord, that so far as we are concerned there is everything that is against Thee and against Thy truth, but we do thank and praise Thee because Thou hast overcome, Thou hast opened the way, Thou hast given us Thy Spirit and Thy Word. So we just trust Thy Spirit and Thy Word to do the work, and we want Thee to truly gain each one of us for Thy own glory. We ask in Thy precious name. Amen.

We are fellowshiping together on this very, very important subject of spiritual submission. I do believe, very much, that this is something to do with the preparation of the bride of the Lamb.

When we think of God, we begin with authority because God is the authority of the universe. His authority is original, it is inherent, it is direct, and His authority must be absolutely submitted to and obeyed. But when we talk about man, I believe that we should not begin with authority. As a matter of fact, we should put that thought of authority far away from our mind. When we mention man, we must begin with submission.

Man's Position In the Universe

What is man? What is man's position in this universe? God created man in His own image after His likeness and after God created man, God gave him dominion over the fowls of the air, the beasts of the field, and the fishes of the sea. In other words, we find that after God created man, He put him above all the other created beings upon this earth. He gave him authority over all these living creatures. So, actually, man is above all, but under

One. Man is created to be above all living creatures. That is the position where God has put him, and yet he is put under the authority of One—that is God. As long as he keeps his position as the one above all but under One, then he is all right. But whenever he forgets that he is under One and remembers only that he is above all, then he is in great trouble. Man is created to submit to God and to obey God. It is only when man submits himself to God that he is able to subdue all things unto God.

I think it is very clear. After God created man and put him in that beautiful garden, the garden of Eden, He gave him one commandment, only one: "Of all the trees in the garden you can freely eat, including the tree of life, but there is one tree, the tree of the knowledge of good and evil, you should not eat because on the day you eat thereof, you shall surely die" (see Genesis 2:15-17).

Why did God give man a commandment? God gave man everything; he could eat of all the trees in the garden of Eden. In the beginning man was a fruit eater, and in the garden of Eden, there were all kinds of fruits. Every fruit was good, and God gave to man bountifully. There were all varieties, all kinds of tastes for man to eat. Best of all, he could even eat of the tree of life; he could even take of God's life. God gave not only all these fruits to man; He even gave Himself to man. He gave everything; only one fruit was forbidden. Why? I believe there are many reasons, but one of the reasons is to remind man that he is under God. He is created to be under the authority of God. That is his position that he must keep. As long as he keeps his position in submitting himself to God, then he can exercise dominion over the fowls of the air, the beasts of the field and the fishes of the sea.

Of course, we know today what happened in the garden of Eden. The enemy tempted Eve. We do not know what really happened, but somehow Eve wandered away from her husband. They should be together. God's will is that they should be one and should not be parted asunder, but somehow, Eve wandered away from Adam. What prompted her to wander away and where was she going? Evidently, she not only wandered away, but there was something in her heart, something she wanted to see, probably out of curiosity. Curiosity is a wonderful thing, but it is also a very terrible thing. Somehow, curiosity caught hold of Eve, and she wandered away from Adam. She went to the tree of the knowledge of good and evil; she looked at the tree, and she began to wonder. That is how everything began.

The Temptation

So, the tempter came and said, "Did God really say that you shall not eat from any of the trees of the garden?" Do you know what he means? Man at that time lived by the fruit of the trees. In other words, if God does not allow them to take the fruit,

God is so cruel. He gives them life and yet He does not allow them to be sustained. So Satan injected a cruel thought into the mind of that curious Eve. Of course, it was not true. Everybody should know that. And yet Satan purposely injected that thought: "Is God so cruel that He created you but without giving you the food that you need?" Of course, Eve would not accept that completely, but somehow you find she accepted something of that evil suggestion because she said, "Oh no, we can eat of all the trees except this one. God said, 'You shall not eat it and you shall not touch it'" (see Genesis 3:1-3). God never said that. It was Eve who added that to it. In other words, God is unreasonable.

So Satan said, "Well, do you know why God did not allow you to eat it? If you eat it, you will know good and evil, and you will be like God. You will be god yourself. You do not need God anymore. God is jealous. He does not want you to be like Him. That is the reason why He forbade you to eat of that tree."

And somehow Eve was deceived. She took the fruit and ate it. In other words, you find she rebelled against the authority of God. She rebelled against God's command. She exerted her self-will. Behind her rebellion is the self-will. She replaced God's will with her own will.

After Eve ate it, probably Adam, came up. He probably was trying to find her. She gave him to eat, and Adam took it. (As a matter of fact, God held Adam responsible. Even though it was the woman who was deceived, God held Adam responsible.) In this rebellious act of Eve, she actually violated two divine orders. First, she violated the divine order of God over man; she rebelled against God, the headship of God. At the same time, she rebelled against God's delegated authority, because in God's divine order, He set the husband as head of the family. So in this one act of Eve, she violated or rebelled against two authorities— God's direct authority and man's indirect authority: God's original authority and man's given authority. She broke both of them, but it was Adam whom God held responsible. Why? When you read Genesis, God said, "You can eat all the fruits except one, the tree of the knowledge of good and evil, because on the day that you eat thereof you shall die." It seems as if that command was given directly to Adam. In the order of Genesis chapter 2, it seems as if Eve was made, was built, after that. So the command was given directly to Adam. Eve heard it from Adam and that is why Adam was more sinful than Eve.

God has made Adam as the head of the family and as the head of the family he was responsible for whatever happened in the family. He should not have allowed Eve to leave him and wander away. He should have taken care of Eve. Somehow he failed in his responsibility over his wife. Eve was deceived, but Adam sinned deliberately. When Eve gave that fruit she had eaten to Adam,

Adam knew very well this was forbidden. He knew very well the consequence; and yet somehow he chose his wife rather than God. He was afraid to lose his wife. He loved his wife so much that he was willing to lose God. It was a deliberate sin, and that is why the Bible says, "Sin entered into this world through one man, and that man was Adam."

The Adamic Nature

"For as in the Adam all die" (I Corinthians 15:22a). After Adam and Eve rebelled against God and exerted their self-will, you find a change in the very life of man. Sin had entered into the world. Sin had contaminated, dominated human life. That human life was corrupted, polluted. That human life had become rebellious and selfish. And in "the Adam" all died. In other words, all who are of Adam, all of us who come out of Adam inherit the Adamic nature and that Adamic nature that we inherit is sinful, corrupted, rebellious, and self-willed. So we need to recognize that rebellion is not something that happened in the beginning of human history; it is not something that happened just once in the garden of Eden. We need to recognize that since that one act of rebellion, rebellion became a nature in human life. We have all inherited that rebellious life. We are all self-willed people. Submission is unknown to us. Obedience is simply not our character. That includes you and me.

The Deception of Outward Appearance

Now, it is true when you try to analyze human beings, you may find that some people seem to be born more submissive, while other people seem to be born more rebellious. But do not be deceived; it is a deception. Even those who seem to be born more submissive than the others are not more submissive. Remember, it is just an outward appearance; it is not real. It can be through custom. For instance, in China because of the long tradition and the custom, you find that the women seem to be more submissive to the men, (but you don't know them). I heard that Chinese women are more strong-willed than men. It is true because of custom or maybe because of education or teaching—Confucius teaching—and because of these things, some kind of a false atmosphere is created that women seem to be more submissive. Well, such submission is unreal. It is suppression. It is painful because inside their heart is boiling.

Furthermore, when people who seem to be very submissive come to the things of God, they are immediately tested. Because there is a natural opposition and a natural rebellion within us, when we come to the things of God, there is a resistance there. We all want our self-will more than God's will. It is natural to us. It is inborn. It is not something taught, it is not something added on; it is inborn. So, we need to recognize this. I think the reason spiritual submission is so rare in this world is because we do not recognize how rebellious we are. We are rebellious beyond remedy, beyond repair. We cannot improve it or cannot educate it. That is the reason why discipline is so necessary.

The Necessity of Discipline

The book of Proverbs is the book of wisdom. Of course, Proverbs deals with human behavior, human relationships. So in Proverbs, many places mention discipline. Why is discipline so necessary? If we are naturally submissive and obedient, we do not need any discipline.

> A rod is for the back of him that is void of understanding (10:13b).
> Folly is bound up in the heart of the child; the rod of correction shall drive it far from him (22:15).
> A whip for the horse, a bridle for the ass, and a rod for the back of fools (26:3).
> The rod and reproof give wisdom; but a child left to himself bringeth his mother to shame (29:15).

Sometimes you wonder why a rod is necessary. Now today, modern minds think the rod is unnecessary. You should not spank your child; you should spare the rod. You should not discipline because human nature is so good, is so perfect. Therefore, you should let it grow, encourage it, and let it freely express itself. Well, you know what happens. Folly is bound up in our hearts and it is only through discipline that it is driven away. So all this shows how important it is for us to realize that in us, that is, in our nature, in our flesh, submission cannot be found. There is no such thing as obedience. It is rebellion. It is self-will. That is why, the sooner we realize this the better. God gave everything to us, and He has only one demand upon us: He only demands submission and obedience. That is all He demands.

Submission and Obedience to God

For our clarity let us try to explain it this way. I think the Chinese words here are marvelous. In Chinese when we talk about this matter of obedience, actually there are two words that represent the two sides of submission and obedience. *Shun* means "obey, follow, do whatever is ordered." It is an act, an action. *Fu* is a matter of a heart attitude; it is "yielding, submitting." Check google translate

Submission is more of an inward attitude. You have an inward attitude to yield, to come under, to be ranked under. And then it should be expressed in action which is obedience. You do whatever you are told to do. Submission without obedience is false. It is pretension, it is unreal, because if there is real submission, there is bound to be obedience. If you have that attitude, it has to be put into practice. But obedience without submission is also unreal. It is just an outward appearance. It is not acceptable.

Do you remember the story our Lord told of two brothers? When the father told the elder son to go and do certain things, that son said he would not do it, but finally he did. When the father told the other son to go and do it, he said he would, but he never did it (see Matthew 21:28-30). So sometimes you may say, "I submit," but you do not do it; it is only in word, not in deed. It is unreal. Sometimes you may be rebellious, but then you repent, and you do it. The important thing for us to see is that to God we need to give absolute submission and absolute obedience. As a matter of fact, God delights in our obedience. The more you obey the more He gives.

Look at Abraham, the father of faith. When the glory of God appeared to Abraham, he obeyed. And in every step of his obedience, God blessed him more and more. When he offered Isaac, God even took an oath on Himself. God's words are eternal and yet God took an oath, as if His words were not enough to reassure Abraham, to bless Abraham.

The book of Job is the first written record in the Bible, chronologically speaking, because the five books of Moses were written by Moses. But Job evidently lived in the time of the Patriarchs, though he was not an Israelite; he was an Edomite. So, there in Job, the first written record in human history, what is the lesson that God wants man to learn? If you read the book of Job, you find God wants Job to learn one lesson and that is submission or obedience. Job was a perfect man. He feared God. He was upright, righteous, very careful, but there was something in him. God knew there was a self-righteousness there. Job was so good that he was self-righteous. So God allowed the tempter to come in and really shake him up and, eventually, he learned the lesson (see Job 42). Job asked, "Why is it that such a good man as I am, so perfect, why is it I suffer so much?" Even though he said, "It is God who gives and God who takes away, blessed be the name of the Lord." Yet somehow within Job's heart there was a murmuring, a complaint. He could not understand. He questioned God. He challenged God to argue with him. God did not argue with Job. His friends argued with him but with wrong arguments. God did not argue with him; all He did was to show him God's glory. And when Job saw God's glory he said, "You are God. You can do anything You like. No one should question You. No one can stand against Your mind. I heard You before; now I see You. I repent in dust and ashes." Job learned a lesson of submission and obedience.

When you come to God, brothers and sisters, you need to know who He is. He is sovereign. You need to see His authority. You need to see His glory. You cannot question Him. All you need to do is submit and obey, to repent in dust and ashes. That is where you are. That is where our position before God is, and it is a blessed position. When Job came to that position, God blessed him with a double portion.

Halfway Obedience

All that God requires of us is obedience. Brothers and sisters, do we give this to Him? When you read I Samuel chapter 15, God commanded Saul through Samuel: "Go and destroy the Amalekites—men and beasts—everything." Why? It was because when the children of Israel came out of Egypt into the wilderness, the Amalekites attacked them and tried to destroy them. You remember the story in Exodus how Joshua fought against them, and Moses went to the mount and raised his hands. While his hands remained raised, Joshua overcame, but when he was tired and his hands came down, then the Amalekites won. So his two hands had to be sustained in order that the Amalekites might be overcome. Since that day, God told Moses, "Write it in the book that the name of the Amalekites shall be wiped out from this world." Of course there is a reason why God commanded this, but we will not go into details. God told Saul: "Go and destroy the Amalekites—men and women and children and beasts—everything."

Saul went. He destroyed the Amalekites and the beasts, but he saved Agag, the king of the Amalekites, and he kept all the best cows and sheep. In other words, he obeyed God only halfway. He thought God was too unreasonable. To destroy the bad is reasonable, but to destroy all the good did not seem right to him. So he kept all the best. He exerted his self-will. He questioned God's authority. He questioned God's wisdom. He thought he was wiser than God. Then Samuel came and Saul had the face [dared] to meet Samuel and say: "I have done all that God has commanded me to do. I have destroyed the Amalekites."

Samuel said, "What do I hear? I hear the bleating, the lowing of the animals. Where did they come from?" "Oh," Saul said, "the people wanted to keep the best things to offer to God, to be devoted to God. If you kill them, they are gone. Why not use them to serve God? The people desired that these things should be kept to serve God."

Then Samuel said, "Does God delight in burnt offerings and sacrifices?" Brothers and sisters, when you come to the things of God, it seems to be our natural tendency that instead of giving God what He desires, we always try to substitute with something else that we think is good.

Burnt Offerings

What is better than burnt offerings? A burnt offering is an offering that burns the whole sacrifice; there is nothing left. If it is a peace offering, you burn something, you give something to the priest, and you keep something for your own enjoyment. But with the burnt offering, the whole sacrifice is burned into ashes for God as God's food. There is nothing higher than a burnt offering. In other words, you are willing to give all to God, the whole animal to God. You are willing to sacrifice, to be deprived of something in order to give to God. We think that is the best, the highest. What can be higher than offering to God a burnt offering? What can be higher than to sacrifice to God? This should please God tremendously. But what is the delight of our God? Does God delight in burnt offerings and sacrifices? The cattle on a thousand hills belong to Him. All these sacrifices belong to Him. Even if you offer to Him, actually it is already His; it is just an expression from us. But does God delight in burnt offerings and sacrifices as to hearkening to His voice? What is God's delight?

Brothers and sisters, we are the redeemed of the Lord; we are supposed to please God. That should be our ambition. The apostle Paul said that he had only one ambition. In II Corinthians chapter 5, in the original he said, "I am ambitious, whether living or dead, I am ambitious to be pleasing to God." Now that should be our heart: to please God, to make God happy, but oftentimes, we try to make God happy with what makes us happy. We do not try to discover God's delight. What does He really want? What will please His heart? What will make Him happy? We fail to discover that. Does God delight in burnt offerings and sacrifices as to hearkening to His voice? In other words, God's delight is that we hear Him, and the "hearing Him" is not just to hear, but also to do. That is what God is delighted with, but how often we try to substitute something else. Isn't it true? When God's will is revealed to us, we try to substitute it with something else.

I remember what happened to our dear brother Watchman Nee. When he was young, he had a girlfriend. They grew up together and he loved her very much. After he was saved, he tried to lead her to the Lord, but he could talk with her about anything under the heaven except the Lord. She would not listen; but he still loved her.

One time he was going to preach, and he was really before the Lord to find a verse. The Lord gave him that verse in Psalm 72: "Whom do I have in heaven but Thee and whom do I desire on earth except Thee?" Brother Nee said he could say, "Whom do I have in heaven but Thee?" He could say that, but he could not say, "Whom do I desire on earth?" Of course, he desired that lady.

Well, he gave the message anyway, but after he gave that message, the Lord dealt with him. So finally one day, the Lord really dealt with him: "Are you willing to follow Me? If you want to be My servant, to be used by Me, if you want to have power to serve Me, you have to follow Me absolutely." He told God, "Just let me have her. I am willing to serve You with double energy. I am willing to go anywhere You want me to go if You just let me have her." He tried to substitute, but God never accepted any substitute. Finally, the love of God touched his heart, and he gave up. And he told us after he gave her up, he changed his clothes, put on an old garment, took some gospel posters, and went to the street and posted them.

It is true with each one of us. I believe you have such times; I do. Whenever God demands obedience, we always try to substitute with sacrifice and burnt offerings. But what God delights in is a hearing heart, to hearken to His voice and to obey.

"Behold, obedience is better than sacrifice, attention than the fat of rams." Why is it that hearkening to the voice of God is better than burnt offerings and sacrifices? It is because obedience is better than sacrifice. It is much better for us to obey than to offer something to Him. Giving Him attention is far better than the fat of rams. We know the fat of rams is the best part of the ram to be burned to God. But God said, "Attention is better."

Why is it that obedience is better than sacrifice? It is because in sacrifice there can still be your self-will, and oftentimes it is. But in obedience your self-will has to be cast aside, and that is the reason why obedience is better than sacrifice, attention is better than the fat of the rams.

Rebellion and Divination

Do we realize how serious rebellion is? Do we really understand the seriousness of self-will? It says, "Rebellion is as the sin of divination." Divination is when you go to a false god, an idol, or you go to some people who are fortune tellers that look at a crystal ball. You go to someone else to seek for counsel for your future and follow it. That is divination, and divination is a sin before God. In the Bible you find it is forbidden, it is an abomination to God. We have God, the true God. He is wisdom. We should go to Him, seek His counsel, find out His will, and do His will. That is what we should do. We should not go outside of our God and seek counsel from man or from idols or from evil spirits. We should not do that. That is an abomination to God. Would you commit the sin of divination? Saul did. You remember, at the very last, Saul went to a witch and tried to find counsel, but God had forbidden him.

Brothers and sisters, if someone said, "You committed the sin of divination," you would say, "No, no I never did that. How can I commit the sin of divination?" But brothers and sisters, rebellion is as the sin of divination. Have you been rebellious? Do we realize the seriousness of it? We make very light of our rebellion and say, "God is so good-natured. He understands. He forgives." But each time we rebel against God, we commit a sin of divination.

Self-Will and Iniquity

"Self-will is as iniquity and idolatry." What is iniquity? Iniquity is violating, trespassing, transgressing the authority, the sovereignty, the glory of God. That is iniquity. Each time we exert our own will we commit iniquity. Any time we exert our will against God's will we commit the sin of idolatry. Do we dare to go and worship an idol? Of course not! But how we dare to be self-willed. Think about this.

The Root of Insubordination

Brothers and sisters, we are dealing with something very fundamental; it is elementary but very fundamental. We need to know where we are. Do you know why we rebel? Do you know why we are unsubmissive? Do you know why we disobey God? Basically, it is because we do not really know who our God is. We say we know who our God is. We say that we know He is sovereign, almighty, our Creator, our God, our Head, our Lord. Mentally, we do, but do we really know who He is? It is not until we rebel that we begin to realize we do not know God as we think we do. The lack of the knowledge of God is the root of our insubordination and disobedience. For us to really submit to God and obey Him, we need to know Him.

Our dear brother Nee said, "Do not count how many times you have obeyed, but count how many times you have disobeyed. Then you know where you are."

The Test of Obedience

The test of our obedience and submission is probably more evident when it comes to this matter of delegated authority. If you really know this is God's direct authority, dare you disobey? You dare not, even though you still do; we all do. But especially when we come to delegated authority, then the test is really severe. In Romans 13:1-7 it says:

Let every soul be subject to the authorities that are above him. For there is no authority except from God; and those that exist are set up by God. So that he that sets himself in opposition to the authority resists the ordinance of God; and they who thus resist shall bring sentence of guilt on themselves. For rulers are not a terror to a good work, but to an evil one. Dost thou desire then not to be afraid of the authority? practice what is good, and thou shalt have praise from it; for it is God's minister to thee for good. But if thou practicest evil, fear; for it bears not the sword in vain; for it is God's minister, an avenger for wrath to him that does evil. Wherefore it is necessary to be subject, not only on account of wrath, but also on account of conscience. For on this account ye pay tribute also; for they are God's

officers, attending continually on this very thing.
Render to all their dues: to whom tribute is due,
tribute; to whom custom, custom; to whom fear,
fear; to whom honor, honor.

Since the time of Noah after the flood, God set
up government in this world because of the evil of
man. God set up government in order to restrain
evil. Whoever sheds the blood, his blood shall be
shed (see Genesis 9:6). That is government. So you
find God has set up government, authorities. God
is the only authority. There is no authority except
from God, so it is God who delegates authority to
those who rule in the government. They are set up
by God for one purpose: to keep order, to punish
the evil, and to protect the good. And because of
this we must submit ourselves to the authorities
that God has set up in this world.

If we really see that authority is of God, then we
shall have no problem because we are not submitting to man, we are submitting to God. Our problem is if we do not know what authority really is,
then we think we are just obeying man or submitting to man and we have great difficulty. When the
authority is right, or we think it is right, then it is
easier for us to submit and to obey. But when we
think the authority is wrong, should we submit
and obey? That is where the difference comes.

If you really understand what authority is, then
you can see. Whether that delegated authority is
right or wrong, if you are under that authority, you

must submit, but it does not mean you must obey. To God you give absolute submission and absolute obedience; to man you can give absolute submission but relative obedience. No human being can demand absolute obedience; that is God's prerogative. We must obey man whom we are under to the extent of our conscience, because our conscience is the voice of God.

Peter and John were preaching Christ. They were taken before the Jewish council, the highest religious authority which they were under. The council forbade these two apostles to preach the gospel and there you find the apostles exhibited a humble spirit, a submissive spirit and said, "To obey God or obey man—which is the right thing to do? We have to obey God. If you want to put us in prison, we will go to prison. We will not rebel, but we cannot obey because we have a higher authority to obey" (see Acts 4:19-20). So this is where the test really is, but we need to recognize God's authority in order to do that.

Dear Lord, we are touching something that is foreign to us. We pray that because Thou hast given us Thy life, Thou will enable us to receive what is from Thee. We pray that Thou will search our hearts and bring us out of ourselves into Christ that we may truly learn submission to know Thy authority. We ask in Thy precious name. Amen.

How Can We Submit?

Ephesians 5:21—Submitting yourselves to one another in the fear of Christ.

Philippians 2:5-11—For let this mind be in you which was also in Christ Jesus; who, subsisting in the form of God, did not esteem it an object of rapine to be on an equality with God; but emptied himself, taking a bondman's form, taking his place in the likeness of men; and having been found in figure as a man, humbled himself, becoming obedient even unto death, and that the death of the cross. Wherefore also God highly exalted him, and granted him a name, that which is above every name, that at the name of Jesus every knee should bow, of heavenly and earthly and infernal beings, and every tongue confess that Jesus Christ is Lord to God the Father's glory.

Hebrews 5:8-10—Though he were Son, he learned obedience from the things which he suffered; and having been perfected, became to all them that obey him, author of eternal salvation; addressed by God as high priest according to the order of Melchisedec.

Dear heavenly Father, we do thank Thee that we who were rebels, sinners, and yet today, in Christ Jesus, we are Thy sons and daughters, Thy very own. It is Thy desire that we shall be conformed to the image of Thy beloved Son, that Thy Son may be the first born among many brethren. Oh, Father, what can we say? It is more than we can even dream of but Thou art doing it by Thy Spirit. So again this morning, as we gather in Thy presence, we offer ourselves to Thee because we are Thy workmanship. We cannot do anything, but Thou will do it all. Lord, we want to hear, we want to cooperate, we want Thee to finish Thy work to the praise of Thy glory. In the name of our Lord Jesus. Amen.

We have been sharing together on this very, very important and needed subject of *Spiritual Submission*. And I do pray to the Lord that it may not be just a subject to talk about. I do look to the Lord who alone is able to make what we are considering together a reality in our lives. To me, I feel it is something that the church of God is very much lacking, and it is probably the biggest reason for all the problems in the church. So I do look to the Lord, that by His Spirit, by His enabling, at least there will be a beginning among His people in this matter of spiritual submission.

We mentioned that we are naturally insubordinate, unsubmissive, and disobedient. In our very nature, that which we have inherited from our father Adam, there is rebellion and self-will. We can see it even in a little baby. It is just in us, and when we talk about submission and obedience, it is foreign to us. It is not in us. Because of our environment, we may outwardly try to appear submissive or even obedient, but we know ourselves, and God knows that it is not real.

Rebellion In Human History

In human history, since the day of Adam's fall, rebellion is the norm. In Genesis chapters 10 and 11, you find that after the flood man began to multiply. You remember God's word to Adam was to multiply and cover the whole earth, to subdue all things unto God. Yet instead of covering the whole earth, as man began to multiply, they wanted to stay together. They refused to cover the whole earth. They wanted to be together for one thing: that they may be able to proclaim their own name.

The Tower of Babel

At that time there was a person whose name was Nimrod and that very name means "rebel." He was a great hunter, a mighty man. He was the first in human history who tried to unite all the people under him and build an empire. Nimrod was an empire builder. So under his leadership, when they moved to the land of Shinar, they built the city of Babylon, and they also started to build the tower of Babel in order to lift up their name. They wanted to build that tower to reach the heavens. God's command was to multiply, to cover the earth, to fulfill the work that God had given to man, to subdue all things, that is, to bring everything back to God. That was man's mission and the reason they were given authority. But unfortunately, instead of serving God's purpose, instead of obeying God's command, they tried to use the power God had given them to build the tower of Babel. It was an open rebellion against the authority of God.

And you remember God said that if man was so united there was nothing they could not do. So God came down and confused their tongues in order to scatter them all over the earth. In one sense it is a judgment, a punishment and even today we suffer for it. We have to have interpretation and translations. But on the other hand, God used it to scatter man to cover the whole earth.

Pharaoh

As you go on in history, when the children of Israel were in Egypt, God sent Moses to deliver His chosen people. Moses faced Pharaoh and said, "God said let My people go that they may serve Me." And Pharaoh said, "Who is Jehovah? I do not know Him. Why should I listen to Him and let the people go?" (see Exodus 5). There is a defiance against God's authority, but very soon judgment fell upon him.

The Children of Israel

The children of Israel were led out of Egypt, but even in the wilderness they rebelled against God. God was so good to them. He took care of them and gave them manna, angel's food, from heaven (see Psalm 78:23-25—NKJV). He gave them the water out of the smitten rock that followed them through the wilderness. He prepared a table in the wilderness. God provided everything for them.

When they came to Kadesh Barnea, the spies came back and said it was indeed a good land but there were giants there. "The people were so tall they looked upon us as grasshoppers. We will be eaten by them; we cannot go in" (see Numbers 13:32-33). So in spite of all that God had shown to them, they rebelled against God. And because of their rebellion, they were not allowed to enter into the Promised Land. They wandered in the wilderness for thirty-eight years until that rebellious generation passed away.

Sennacherib and Nebuchadnezzar

When you come to the books of Kings and Chronicles, you find Sennacherib, king of Assyria. He sent his emissary to blaspheme against the Lord, and the Lord sent an angel and killed the army (see II Kings 18:13, 19:35-37). Then you find Nebuchadnezzar, the king of Babylon. Because of his pride, he felt he was the one who built that wonderful city of Babylon. And punishment fell upon him until he realized that the heavens do rule over the affairs of men (see Daniel 4:28-32).

Rebellion Against God's Delegated Authority

All these show that rebellion is the very character of mankind. Submission and obedience are totally unknown. There is not only rebellion against God's direct authority, but there are many instances of rebellion against God's delegated authority. Even to our days, you find the children rising up against their parents and being disobedient to them, the students rising up against their teachers, the employees against their employers, and the people against their government. Rebellion and self-will is the very nature of human beings.

Even among the children of Israel, there were those who rebelled against God's delegated authority. For instance, Korah, Dathan, Abiram, and two hundred and fifty of the leaders of the children of Israel rebelled against Moses and Aaron and said, "You usurp the authority. All the people of God are holy; why do you set yourself up above the congregation of the Lord?" And you remember, Moses and Aaron bowed and laid their faces upon the earth, and God came forth to vindicate Himself (see Numbers 16:1-40).

Even in the New Testament, the same thing happened. When John the Baptist was sent by God to preach repentance, the priests, the scribes, the Pharisees, the ecclesiastical authority sent messengers to John, asking who gave him such authority: "Who are you? We are the authority. Now who are you?" And they even questioned our Lord Jesus: "Who gives You the authority to cleanse the temple? Who are You after all?" So, the religious, ecclesiastical authority is always against the spiritual authority of God. That which is positional is always against that which is of life.

Not only that, you find rebellion even against God's delegated authority. You remember how God used Paul to bring the church in Corinth into being, and yet in Corinth there were people questioning his apostolic authority.

So, brothers and sisters, in human history, you will find that rebellion and self-will is the norm because that is what man is. Obedience, submission is foreign; it is not there. But I do not think that we need to use many instances in order to prove how rebellious we are. I think we know ourselves. We do not need to look into history to know that, just look within yourself. If we just recall our own very short history, and you can see that obedience is just not there.

Why do we spend time in telling each other how rebellious we are? how self-willed we are? Why do we do that? We all know it. We have to do it because even though we know it, yet we do not know it. In other words, we refuse to accept it. We think that we can be obedient. We think that we are submissive. We even think that our rebellion is just occasional, our self-will is just "under the weather," but we are an obedient and submissive people. After we are saved, we think we have totally changed; but have we changed? Are we changed?

Today, the reason submission is so rare, the reason obedience is almost unknown in the church of God is because we have a wrong concept. We think we have changed after we believed in the Lord Jesus. Remember, Adam never changes. That which is born of the flesh is flesh. As long as the flesh is in you, rebellion and self-will is always present. You have not changed. This is the first thing we have to come to accept.

Brothers and sisters, if we expect deliverance, if we really expect to be submissive and obedient, then first of all we have to come to the point to realize, to acknowledge, to confess that there is no submission and obedience in us, that is, in our flesh. Have we come to that point? If we have not come to that point, there is no deliverance. We need to ask the Lord to open our eyes to really see it. It is very strange; we think we see, and yet we do not see it.

We have mentioned Job. Job had to go through such hard experience in order to come to the place where he could see. We all need that. We need God to open our eyes, give us a revelation to really see that in us, that is in our flesh, there is no good, no submission, no obedience—nothing.

The Second Man

Throughout human history, all you find upon this earth is rebellion and self-will; until one day, God sent His only beloved Son into this world to be a man. In the first man, in the first Adam, there is no hope. He cannot be improved, educated, instructed, or developed. There is no hope. So God sent us the second Man, even our Lord Jesus.

We have mentioned Philippians chapter 2 a number of times because this is where our salvation comes. Philippians chapter 2 tells us that our Lord Jesus, as the Son of God, is equal with God. In the Godhead we have the Father, the Son, and the Holy Spirit. It is a mystery—three in one, one in three. We cannot explain it. We believe it because we find it is revealed in the word of God. Even though the word "trinity" is not there, the fact, the reality is there. The Godhead is made up of the Father, the Son, and the Holy Spirit, and the three are equal. The Son is equal with the Father, equal in everything. Among the Godhead there is no front, no back, no above, no beneath, no high, no low. They are equal. And the glory of the Godhead is authority. That is the glory of God. Submission and obedience are unthinkable when you think of God. Who should He submit to? Who should He obey? He is to be obeyed, to be submitted to. He is the Sovereign, the Authority of the universe. That is God. So remember, in the Godhead the glory is authority. Obedience is un-known; it is not necessary.

I dare not go too deeply into the mystery of the Godhead, but if you allow me, I will try to throw out a thought and if it is wrong, forgive me. In the beginning, in the Godhead, there is no concept of submission or obedience — only authority. I believe we can all accept that. Now I wonder, when does submission come in? To use human words, there was a council. In eternity past, before anything was created, there was only God — eternally existent, self-existent. But somehow, to use human words, there must have been a kind of council among the Godhead. Of course, that council was different. We have to talk to have a council, but God does not need that. So somehow, there was a council among the Godhead.

The Father loved the Son so much, He wanted to glorify His Son. Love always looks for an outlet. The Father loves the Son so much He wants to give something to His Son, to glorify His Son. He wants to create all things and give all things to His Son, to make His Son heir of all things. He wants to give man to His Son, to be created in His own image, after His likeness, that man may have fellowship, communion with Him and be united with Him in life, in love, in purpose and share His Son's glory and responsibility. Now, these are the glorious thoughts of the Father concerning His Son. But be-ing omniscient, He knows the end from the very beginning. He knew that there would be problems, not only with the unseen world, the angelic beings, but there would be problems with the visible world, even with man who was to be created.

The Lamb of God

May I say, there was a hesitation: "Should We do it? Or should We not?" And during that period, the Son stepped forward. He loved His Father so much, He wanted His Father's will to be done. He wanted to please His Father. He wanted to satisfy His Father's heart. So He stepped forward and said, "Father, if this is what You want, this is what I want. I am willing to offer Myself as the Lamb so that Your will might be done." There was perfect agreement in the Godhead. Our Lord Jesus is called the Lamb slain *from* the foundation of the world, not *before* the foundation of the world. Sometimes, in our chorus it says, "a Lamb slain before the foundation of the world." You do not find that in the Scripture. It is "from the foundation of the world."

So, the Lamb figure is a figure of submission. I wonder whether this spirit of submission began at that time because it is in the spirit of submission that our Lord Jesus, the Son of God, emptied Himself. "He who was equal with God, and that was not something to be grasped at." You know, there was one who tried to grasp that equality with God—Lucifer the archangel; but it was not his. But here you find the eternal Son was equal with God, it was not something to be grasped at because it was His right. From the very beginning, it was His. He was in the form of God.

The Form of God

What is the form of God? The form of God is the manifestation of the fullness of deity, of the fullness of the glory of deity. He subsists in the form of God and yet He emptied Himself. In emptying Himself, you see the spirit of submission. In order to submit Himself to the Father's will, He laid aside the glory, the honor, the power, the authority, the position of God. He laid all these aside. Of course, He cannot empty Himself of His deity. That is impossible because that is what He is, eternally is; it never changes. From the beginning, He is God. When He came to become a man, He is still God. After He returned to heaven, He is God. And into eternity to come, He is God. That is what He is. That is His very being. He cannot empty that, but He was able to empty all the glory and honor associated with deity. He emptied all these.

He laid aside His omnipotence. He is almighty God and yet He laid this aside to become a helpless babe. He laid aside His omniscience—knowing everything. He said, "I do not know; My Father is the only One who knows." He laid aside His omnipresence. He is everywhere at all times, but He came to become a man. When He was in Judea, He was not in Galilee. He laid aside His glory to be worshiped; instead He put Himself under.

So brothers and sisters, here you find our Lord Jesus brought the spirit of submission into this world. He took upon Himself the form of a bondslave. In other words, instead of the form of God, manifesting the full glory of deity, He took up another form. He took up a form that would manifest the fullness of lowliness—no right of His own, worse than anybody else, under everybody—a bondslave. He became a man, and being in figure as a man, He humbled Himself.

What is the glory of God? The glory of God is authority. When God's authority is manifested, you see glory. What is the glory of man? The glory of man is submission and obedience. Whenever that appears, there is glory.

He Took the Form of Man

When our Lord Jesus was born as a man, He took upon Himself the form of a man, human flesh. He is just like we are, but with this difference: in our human flesh, there is sin because we inherited that sinful human nature from Adam. But in the human flesh of our Lord Jesus, there is no sin because He does not come from Adam. It was the Holy Spirit who overshadowed the womb of a virgin. So when He was born, He was called "the holy Thing" (see Luke 1:35). Yes, our Lord Jesus took upon Himself a human flesh. Because we are flesh and blood, therefore He partook of flesh and blood in order to be one with us, but remember, in His human flesh there is no sin. His human flesh is perfect.

He Became Obedient

May I put it another way? Even the self of our Lord Jesus is perfect. If He wanted to exert His own self, there is no sin there. But brothers and sisters, He humbled Himself becoming obedient. You know, obedience is not in God. The Son had to learn obedience from the things which He suffered. He came with a spirit of submission to submit Himself willingly, joyfully to His Father. While He was on earth, He took God as His Head. In the Godhead, there is no head or body. They are one, equal; no above and below. They are equal. But in the spirit of submission, He emptied Himself. He took upon Himself a human flesh. He stood in the place of man before God. The place of man before God is submission.

He Took the Place of Man

Adam did not take his place before God, and here the second Man came and took the place of man, as man ought to be. In that spirit of submission He took the place of man. He submitted Himself to God His Father throughout His life. During those thirty-three years, there was not a single instance that He was not submissive. He said that He could not do anything by Himself. He did it because He saw His Father doing it. That is His Father's will. He could not even say anything. He said it because He heard His Father saying it. It was His Father who spoke within Him. He said, "My time is not yet come, but your time is always ready" (John 7:6). Every minute of His life was governed by God's will. He was submissive to the uttermost—absolute submission.

Being a perfect man, His will is perfect, His mind is clear, His emotion is pure. If He exercises His own will and wills something for Himself, there is nothing wrong with that; it is always right. If He thinks of anything on His own, it is always clear. If He expresses Himself in His emotion, it is pure. No sin will be involved. And yet even with that sinless, perfect flesh—self—He laid down His flesh. He laid down His self: "Not my will but Thy will be done."

Even though His will is perfect, He laid down His will. We think that if what we will to do is good, that should be all right. We do not think that we need to lay down our good will, we only need to lay down our bad will. But here you find our Lord Jesus laid down His perfect will: "Not my will but Thy will be done."

How His emotion was completely yielded, subordinated unto God, even with His mother whom He loved so much and cared for so much. When she wanted Him to do something on His own, He said, "Little woman, what have I to do with you?" (see John 2:2-4). Throughout His life, He walked the way of the cross. He suffered.

Brothers and sisters, we cannot imagine the sufferings of our Lord as a man. We are dull, we are not sensitive, we are not pure; and because that is what we are, we do not suffer as much as our Lord Jesus. There are many things that we are not even aware of. People could go into the temple, day after day, year after year, and see all these people selling and buying in the temple area, and everybody said, "That is the way it ought to be. It is for convenience sake; it is for expedience sake." Nobody felt hurt; but our Lord was hurt, deeply hurt because He was pure. He was the perfect Man.

I cannot imagine how much He suffered. He suffered misunderstanding from the world. He suffered from His own disciples. They could not understand Him. He tried to help them throughout the years and at the very last they still did not understand. What sufferings! But from the things which He suffered; He learned one thing—*obedience*. The spirit of submission becomes the action of obedience through the cross, through suffering.

Becoming obedient is not what He was before. He was the authority. He had to learn obedience in the way of suffering. Our dear brother Nee says, "Becoming obedient is seeking every opportunity to submit and to obey." It is not just when the environment is right that you submit and obey. At all times you look for an opportunity for submission; you look for obedience.

Our Lord Jesus was sent by God into this world to re-establish God's authority on this earth. He was sent by God to this earth to recover the authority of God on earth, to establish the kingdom of God on earth. Oh, but when He was on earth, He never claimed to be authority. He did not try to establish His authority. He came to demonstrate submission and obedience. He sought every opportunity to submit and to obey. That is the life of our Lord Jesus. He came out from heaven, from the Godhead, as it were, but He refused to return to the Godhead in His deity. Once He came out, He will never return to the Godhead in His deity alone. He will return in the way of submission and obedience. That is the way He returned to His Father. No wonder the Father highly exalted Him and gave Him a name that is above every name, and to that name every knee shall bow, every tongue confess that Jesus is Lord.

True Submission and Obedience

It is our Lord Jesus who brought submission and obedience into this world. For the first time in human history, we begin to see what submission and obedience really are in God's thought. But thank God, He learned obedience not just for Himself. In Hebrews 5:8 we are told: "Though He were Son, He learned obedience from the things which

He suffered; and having been perfected ..." Oh, He is perfected—perfect in submission and obedience! That is the kind of submission and obedience that God is looking for in man from the very beginning. "… and having been perfected, became to all them that obey him, author of eternal salvation; addressed by God as high priest according to the order of Melchisedec" (Hebrews 5:9-10).

In I Corinthians 15:22 it says, "in the Adam all die." What a tragedy! We all became rebellious and self-willed people. We cannot help it, but in Christ we have all been made alive.

Do you realize that when you believe in the Lord Jesus, something has happened in you, something far, far greater than having your sins forgiven? That is great, but it is something even greater than the guarantee of going to heaven. When you believe in the Lord Jesus, do you see that you receive a new life?

Now what is that life? We call it eternal life. By eternal life, we think it is just life that continues on endlessly, which is true. But eternal life is a different kind of life. There is a quality of life there. Are you satisfied with your quality of life today? Are you willing to have this kind of life continue forever? Well, when you are young, you want to live, but when you get older, you become too tired to live.

When we believe in the Lord Jesus, He gives us His own life. What is that life? We always think of that life as the life of God. Yes, it is God's uncreated life that is given to us with all the potentials there. But remember, that Life has come into this earth and lived for thirty-three years, and has learned obedience. In other words, the life that we receive from our Lord Jesus, the life in you and in me, this new life is none other than our Lord Jesus Himself. In that life there is submission; in that life there is obedience. We cannot find submission and obedience anywhere else. It is all in a life and that life has been given to us. Oh, brothers and sisters, what love! Praise God, now, by His nature, we are submissive. Do you know that? What was not there before is now present. What was impossible before is now possible. According to that new life we cannot but be submissive; we cannot but obey. We cannot rebel. We cannot exert our self-will. It is not there.

Unfortunately, we do not know what we have. Unfortunately, we still live on that old life that should have been discarded long ago. We do not know how to live by this new life in us. When we submit, we feel happy. Isn't that true? When we rebel, we feel sad. It is because we have a new life now and that life is submissive. Why do we not live a joyful life? Why must we live such a poor life by being rebellious? That is the difference between a Christian and an unbeliever. To an unbeliever rebellion is natural, easy, happy, and joyful; but to a Christian rebellion is unnatural, painful, and hurtful. Unless we repent we cannot get over it; we are grieved. The very life that is in us is a submissive, obedient life. Brothers and sisters, why not live by that life? It is yours.

Let me try another angle. God has never withdrawn His authority from the universe. Do you know that? Yes, there was rebellion everywhere, everyday; but does that mean God has withdrawn His authority from the universe? He has not. Not only has He not withdrawn His authority from the universe, but He is going to establish His authority upon this earth among men. He is working to recover His kingdom on this earth. That is what God is doing. That is the reason why He sent His Son into this world. Our Lord Jesus came into this world to re-establish God's authority. And the way He establishes God's authority is by submission and obedience. In this rebellious world, you find our Lord Jesus is the kingdom of God. In His life God's authority is re-established; He is the obedient One.

Now, God has gotten a people through the redemption of our Lord Jesus. Who are we? We are the redeemed of the Lord, and as the redeemed of the Lord, as the church of God, do we know that it is in the church of God that God is to re-establish His authority and obedience? Then through the obedience of the church to the authority of God, God is to recover the whole earth.

The Character of God's House

So what is the church? Brother Sparks said: "Subjection is the principle of the house in the building of His temple. Submission is a divine law. It is the appointed way of the redeemed ones. It is the way to the throne." He also said: "God models the church on the principle of subjection. Every one in the house of God must learn to submit, to be in subjection. The whole church needs to be in subjection to the authority of the Holy Spirit. We all need to learn submission and obedience to God. Even those who are given authority need to learn subjection to the authority of God."

May I put it another way. The first thing to learn when you come into the church is submission. Do not come to the house of God and ask, "Over whom do I have authority?" Instead, come to the house of God and ask, "To whom should I submit?"

Take the body as an illustration. The head is the authority, and Christ is the Head. He is the authority. The whole body has to subject itself to the Head. Only when the body is in subjection to the Head can the body function. So what is the glory of the body? The glory of the body is submission and obedience. That is what the body is. We are members of one another. As members of one another, the first thing we have to think about is the first law that governs the body. It is not authority; it is obedience. The body has to obey the head.

Only by holding fast the Head, will the whole body be connected together, and minister one to another, and increase with the increase of God. So, remember that in the body the first question is never authority. In the body, the first question is submission and obedience.

All the members of the body are in subjection to the Head. Everyone has to hold fast the Head, Christ, then you find all the members of the body submit to one another. Now it is true that every member of the body is delegated, is given, a certain measure of authority. The Head does delegate, does give authority to every member of the body. There is a measure of authority in every member of the body. That is why you submit to one another in the fear of Christ. You may ask, "Why should I submit to this brother or that sister? We are equal." Well, in one sense we are; we are members one of another. But in another sense, you find that in each member there is a measure of authority put in by the Head. In each member there is a measure of Christ there, and where Christ is, there is authority.

Authority is not you or me; authority is God, is Christ. It is that life. In that life there is a measure of authority. So why is it we need to submit to one another? Sometimes we say, "The sisters should submit to the brothers." Well, the brothers need to submit to the sisters too, in the fear of Christ. It is not because you are a brother, not because you are a sister, not because of anything else; it is because there is Christ in you. When Christ is expressed in you, I have to submit. Even if you are the smallest member of the body of Christ, even if you were just saved an hour ago, if Christ is manifested in you, we have to obey. We obey Christ, we do not obey man.

"In the fear of Christ." Now, the word *fear* is not the fear of being punished; it is a holy fear. When you really love a person, there is a fear there. You are afraid you may not please him or please her. You want to do everything to please him; that is fear. And we want to do everything to please Christ. Brothers and sisters, when we see Christ in a brother or sister, we want to please that Christ there. We are not men-pleasers; instead, we want to please Christ. And in order to please Christ, we need to submit.

Submission should be the character of God's house. Unfortunately, in the church today, there is struggling, fighting for power, for authority, for position. That is not what the church is. The character of the church is submission, is obedience. When you come to the house of God, you should find the beauty of submission there.

Submit to one another in the fear of Christ, and out of this submission, the divine order in the house is established. It is on the basis of submitting to one another in the fear of Christ, as we find in Ephesians 5:21, that it can be followed by verse 22 and onward: Wives, submit yourselves to your own husbands; husbands, love your own wives;

children, obey your parents; parents, do not offend your children; servants, obey your masters; masters, do not ill-treat your servants. In other words, all the other submission and obedience comes out from this one. If we do not know how to submit to one another in the fear of Christ, there will be no authority and submission in our family. There will be no authority and submission in the place where we work. There will be no authority in society or in the world. There will be none.

Exhibiting the Spirit of Submission

So, brothers and sisters, what should we do? Are you willing to lay aside your quest for authority? Are you willing to take up the Spirit of the Lamb, the Spirit of Christ? It is there. It is a matter of whether you are willing to let that life live. You have stifled that life; that life has suffered. Are you willing to release it? Are you willing to take a stand? Are you willing to say, " I want to live by the life of Christ in me, that is, I want to exhibit the spirit of submission. I want to have the mind of Christ"? You have the mind of Christ. The only thing is, are you willing?

I do hope there will be a change of atmosphere in the church. Brothers and sisters, I have to weep when I see how God's people fight for power, for authority, and for position. That is not what the church is. Where can you see the spirit of submission? Where can you see that readiness to obey in the church? Where can you see Christ?

Now it is true, for that spirit of submission to be translated into acts of obedience you have to suffer. Our Lord Jesus came with a spirit of submission, and in that spirit, He was able to learn obedience. If you do not have the spirit of submission, you will never learn obedience—never. But if you have that spirit of submission, then you will begin to learn how to obey. But when you begin to learn how to obey, you will suffer because the flesh in you is not willing. Your flesh will suffer.

Christian experience is a paradox. If you follow the flesh, the flesh is happy, but the spirit is sad. But if you follow the spirit, the spirit is happy, but your flesh is groaning. It is only when you are willing to be yoked with Christ, you have the spirit of submission. To be yoked with Christ is an act of will. The yoke is heavy, in a sense, upon your neck, so you lose your freedom. Not until you are willing to put your neck under that yoke of Christ to be equally yoked with Him in the spirit of submission, will you begin to learn from Christ how lowly and meek He is. Whenever you want to go your own way, whenever your flesh wants to raise its head, whenever your self-will wants to exert itself, the Holy Spirit will remind you. That prick will gently touch you and you will understand. It is only by way of the cross that submission can be turned into obedience. This is the way our Lord Jesus has gone through, and this is the way He has opened for us. If we do not have His life in us, we cannot walk this way, but thank God, with His life in us, He is going through with us. Or to put it another way, He is carrying us through.

Oh, brothers and sisters, my prayer is there will be a change of spirit among God's people, that we will see more of the spirit of submission and the actions of obedience. If you cannot find this in the church, where else can you find it? If the Lord is not able to bring us to that place, how is He going to establish His authority in the universe? And only when you really enter into the spirit of submission can you begin to appreciate God's delegated authority.

You know why you do not appreciate God's delegated authority in the church? It is because the spirit of submission is not there. If the spirit of submission is in you, you will appreciate those brothers and sisters whom the Lord has put above you, as it were, to take care of you. How they labor for your soul! You appreciate them. What a difference it will be!

Today, everywhere in the church, you find brothers and sisters rebelling against delegated authority. But oh, once you see and you come into a spirit of submission, you thank God for those brothers and sisters to whom God has given authority to serve you, to care for you. What a difference it would make! I know only the Spirit of God is able to bring us there. Let us look to Him.

Dear heavenly Father, we do thank Thee Thou has gotten the Man. We thank Thee that Thy beloved Son is willing to submit Himself to Thee and to learn obedience from the things which He suffered, that He might become the Author of our eternal salvation. Oh, teach us how to obey Him. Thou art our High Priest in the order of Melchisedec. Support us with Thy life that we may be able to really enter into submission and obedience that Thy authority may be established in this universe. Glory to God! In the name of our Lord Jesus. Amen.

Questions on Spiritual Submission

Question #1 – Could you please explain, in a practical way, how we submit ourselves without obeying?

Now if we want to find a way out of obeying, then I feel sorry about it. If we really have a spirit of submission, if we are ready to obey, that will be the right attitude. I hope it is not an escape kind of question, but I hope it is a real question.

May I put it this way? If the Lord really gives us a spirit of submission, then we are ready to obey because submission that is not ready to obey is false. In this world, we have many examples. Outwardly, we may submit, but actually that kind of submission is false, is not from within. It is being pressed and it is not willing or joyful. So when we consider this matter of spiritual submission, actually, what we mean is the spirit of Christ is in us. Because His Spirit is a spirit of submission, therefore it is a voluntary, willing, and joyful thing. It is something within; it is not something outward.

I remember in one of Brother Nee's writings (I do not think it is in English yet), he mentioned that in this world the whole matter of authority and obedience is external. It is objective; it is not something within. When you exercise authority, it is a position, and when you obey an authority, it is just an objective thing. It is not something subjective.

But when we really come to the Lord, the whole thing has changed. Instead of being objective, it has become subjective. Submission becomes something from within and obedience is the same way. You do not just obey an outward authority. You are obeying God. Everything becomes subjective and that is real. So if we really have a spirit of submission, I hope that we are ready to obey.

But there are occasions when we find that we can submit but we cannot obey. Now this applies only to man; it does not apply to God. When you come to God, it is absolute submission and absolute obedience. Never think of trying to submit without obeying, or obeying without submitting. To God it is absolute submission and absolute obedience. However, man's authority is given, it is not original; man's authority is indirect, not direct. Man's authority is to represent God, so whenever delegated authority misrepresents God, then you have this problem. If God has put you under such authority, whether it represents or misrepresents God, you must submit. For instance, the government is set up by God. It should represent God to protect the good and to punish the evil. That is what government is for. But suppose a government misrepresents God, then what do you do? As long as you are under that government, you have to submit, but when the government tries to ask you to do something against God, against your conscience, then you have a higher authority to obey. In other words, you still obey. It does not mean you do not need to obey, but you obey the higher authority. You obey God.

The practical instances we find in Scripture are in the book of Acts. Remember in Acts chapter 4, after that lame man was healed, many people surrounded Peter and John, and Peter began to preach Christ to them. As he was preaching Christ to them, they were taken to the ecclesiastical authority represented by the high priest and so forth. Since they were Jews, they were under that ecclesiastical council, and when they were brought before that council, they were forbidden to preach Christ. So Peter and John said, "To obey you or to obey God, which is the right thing? But we have to preach Christ." Their attitude was submissive. They did not rebel. They were willing to be punished, and yet they had to obey God.

In Acts chapter 5, the same thing happened. The twelve apostles were preaching and again they were taken to the council. They were forbidden to preach, and their answer was: "We must obey God rather than man." So it is in this kind of situation that you submit and yet you do not obey. It does not mean you do not obey completely; it means that you obey the higher authority. So obedience is still there.

Or to use another illustration, in the family, your parents are God's delegated authority. That is the reason why you find the Scripture says, "Children, obey your parents in all things" (Colossians 3:20). Now suppose your parents order you to steal or to kill, what will you do? Or suppose your parents order you to give up your faith in Christ Jesus, what will you do? You need to maintain a submissive attitude. You should not fight against your parents; you should not exhibit a defiant spirit. You should still be submissive because they are your parents, God's delegated authority over you. You are still under that authority, but you can gently, softly say, "I am sorry, I cannot do it because it is against God's will." Now if your parents want to punish you, meekly accept the punishment, and that is submission without giving them obedience because you are giving obedience to your higher authority. So you really cannot separate submission and obedience. As a matter of fact, there is no way to submit and not obey. If you submit, you have to obey, but whom are you obeying? That is the real question.

Question #2 – Why is it significant that the Lamb was slain *from* the foundation of the world and not *before* the foundation of the world?

This is a theological question. Even though it is a theological question, I think it is very important because we find that the Holy Spirit is very careful in the use of words. We are very careless, but God is very careful, and the word of God is breathed by God. So every word that is used is carefully used. The Lord Jesus is called the Lamb slain from the foundation of the world, and that is the only descriptive phrase used in the New Testament. We do not find anywhere in the New Testament that He is the Lamb slain before the foundation of the world.

What is the difference? Before the foundation of the world, according to Ephesians, God purposed in Himself a purpose and that purpose is to sum up all things in Christ. That is God's eternal purpose. Now in that purpose, God is to create all things, to give all things to His Son that His Son may have the preeminence over all things. That is God's purpose before the foundation of the world. In that purpose, God had not purposed that man would fall into sin. Do you see the difference? If God had purposed that man would fall into sin and He purposed that His Son would come to be the Lamb to redeem man, then we would say that we are not responsible for our fall; God is responsible because He purposed it that way. So remember, redemption is not in the purpose of God. The purpose of God is the glorification of the Son, the exaltation of the Son, the preeminence of the Son. That is God's purpose.

But after God had purposed that purpose, He had a problem. Because He is omniscient, He knows the future, He knows the end from the beginning. To Him there is no past or future; it is always present because God is eternal. So after God had purposed that purpose and He saw that problem (then, as we try to use human words to explain it), then the Son stepped forward and said, "Father, go ahead. I am willing to be that Lamb." So the Lamb cannot be slain before the foundation of the world. In other words, before the world was created, before man was created, how could the Lamb be slain? There was no use for it. It is only after God created mankind, then there is the need of the Lamb to be slain. That is why the Scripture always puts it this way: "He is the Lamb slain from the foundation of the world." After the world was created, then there was the need for the Lamb to be slain.

I think the important thing to notice is that it is not just a play on words. If it were just a play on words, we could ignore it, but there is a real and basic truth in it. Of course, to us redemption is everything because we are self-centered, but to God redemption is actually a remedial measure; it is not God's original purpose. God's original purpose is centered upon His Son.

Question #3 – Please elaborate more on this verse: "Go and utterly destroy the Amalekites, and fight against them until they be consumed" (I Samuel 15:18).

> And Amalek came and fought with Israel in Rephidim. And Moses said to Joshua, Choose us men, and go out, fight with Amalek; to-morrow I will stand on the top of the hill with the staff of God in my hand. And Joshua did as Moses had

said to him, to fight with Amalek; and Moses, Aaron and Hur went up to the top of the hill. And it came to pass when Moses raised his hand, that Israel prevailed; and when he let down his hand, Amalek prevailed. And Moses' hands were heavy; then they took a stone, and put it under him, and he sat on it; and Aaron and Hur supported his hands, one on this side, and one on that side; and his hands were steady until the going down of the sun. And Joshua broke the power of Amalek and his people with the edge of the sword. And Jehovah said to Moses, Write this for a memorial in the book, and rehearse it in the ears of Joshua, that I will utterly blot out the remembrance of Amalek from under the heavens. And Moses built an altar, and called the name of it Jehovah-nissi. And he said, For the hand is on the throne of Jah; Jehovah will have war with Amalek from generation to generation (Exodus 17:8-16).

I mentioned that when the children of Israel came out of Egypt, the first enemy they met was the Amalekites. God had delivered His people out of Egypt to bring them into the Promised Land, but the enemy came and tried to destroy them on the way. In other words, the hand of the enemy is not only upon the children of Israel, his hand is against the throne of God. He wants to frustrate, to destroy God's will for His people. Now, the enemy was so strong Joshua could not overcome them. But thank

God, through the intercessory prayer of Moses, he prevailed against the enemy. So after that incident, God said, "Write it down. I will blot out the name of the Amalekites from the earth." It says that the hand is upon the throne of Jehovah; Jehovah will have war with Amalek generation to generation. That is the background.

With that background, in the days of Saul, God gave Saul a command: "Go and destroy the Amalekites." Saul went only halfway because he felt that it was a pity to destroy all the fatted cows and sheep. He destroyed all the people, but he left the best. He spared the king of the Amalekites, Agag, and he spared all the best of the animals. So that is why God said, "Does God delight in burnt offering and sacrifices, as in hearkening to His voice?"

So the Amalekites represent the flesh. The hand of the flesh is always raised against God. And God is at war with the flesh, even today. As long as we allow the flesh to remain, we find it is against the spirit. The mind of the flesh is against the mind of the spirit, and as long as you allow the flesh to dominate you, your spirit suffers. You will not be able to arrive at God's purpose into Canaan Land, into the fullness of Christ. You will not be allowed to. And you find it is very true in our personal experience. The greatest enemy is not outside of you; the greatest enemy is the one within you. So Martin Luther said, "I am not afraid of the Pope, but I am afraid of the pope within me."

The flesh has to be dealt with. We cannot allow it to remain. What we always do is just allow the best to remain. We agree to kill the bad flesh, but we want to offer the good flesh to God to serve God. Isn't that what we are all doing? But as long as we allow the good flesh to remain, flesh is flesh and the bad will come out too. It never changes. He that is born of the flesh is flesh.

In typology and also in actuality, you find God's law is that the flesh must go, must be wiped out from generation to generation, to the end. You have to, by the Spirit of God, put the flesh to death from generation to generation all the time. You do not know when the flesh will come out. But thank God, whenever it comes out, the Holy Spirit will remind you and then you deliver it unto death.

So, it is very important that the Amalekites must be destroyed. And you remember, because Saul spared Agag, the result was that he was killed by a son of the Amalekites. Of course, there are other instances in the Scripture, but we do not need to go into it. Is there any meaning in I Samuel 15:33: "Samuel put Agag to death"? It is evident. Samuel stood with God; he obeyed. He gave his attention to God and because of that, he finished the work that Saul failed to do.

Question #4 – "Delight in the Lord."
In service to the Lord, how do you know that He is delighted?

First of all, it is very important that we live, or we serve to please the Lord. It was Paul's ambition, and it is our ambition as Christians. Some people say after you become a Christian, you cannot be ambitious, therefore you are finished. In this world, you need to be ambitious to accomplish anything. But do you know that we Christians are the most ambitious people in the world? Yes, we are not ambitious for the things of the world because we know they are but refuse, but we are ambitious to please our Lord. No ambition can be higher than that and no ambition is harder to achieve than that. You have to put your whole being into it. It must occupy your whole being in order to fulfill that ambition. And that ambition never comes to an end.

In this world, you may be ambitious to achieve a certain scholastic achievement and then you get it. But after you get it, then what? It is a great let down. But if you are ambitious to please the Lord, your ambition increases all the time. It never comes to an end. Wonderful! So, our whole being is to please Him.

Look at the Lord Jesus. "This is My beloved Son in whom is My delight." And He wants us to be like His own Son. Of course, we know the only possibility is by His life in us, not by ourselves.

In service to the Lord, how do you know He is delighted? **Number one:** You know He is delighted if your service is His will. **Number two:** You know He is delighted if you are doing that service in the power of the Holy Spirit and not with your own strength or wisdom. **Number three:** You know He is delighted because you sense the anointing upon you. You sense His presence with you. It is not measured by what people say, it is not even measured by the result. It is measured by His presence, by His anointing. You may serve faithfully for ten years with no result, but if the presence of the Lord is there, you know He is delighted. You may have great results, great success because you are very capable, but if the presence of the Lord is not with you, it is of zero value. So that is how we know.

Question #5 – Service can get into a routine every week. How can we renew and delight the Lord?

Now it is true, there is always that danger. It can be the will of God, it can be that you are doing it by the power of the Holy Spirit, and the Lord is with you, but when it becomes a routine, there is always the danger of gradually losing that touch with the Lord. You begin to feel that you know how to do it. So it may start in the will of God, start in His power, start with His presence, but when it becomes a routine, there is always the danger of losing that contact with the Lord, and you are on your own. How do we renew that? To renew it you have to return to the Lord. Each time you touch a routine, touch it with a fresh contact with the Lord.

If there is that fresh contact with the Lord, every routine is new. You do not need to change. We often say after a thing has been done a number of times it gets old, and you get tired of it, so you have to invent a new way for stimulation. Now the flesh needs that, but the spirit does not need that. Even a routine can be living and new as long as there is life there, as long as there is the Spirit there. So you need to always keep in touch with the Lord. Never come to a point where you feel like you can do it now. As a matter of fact, the more you do it, the more you find you cannot do it. So that is important.

Question #6 – In new decisions in service, how do we know that will delight the Lord?

Of course, you need to seek the Lord and to see that it is His will.

TITLES AVAILABLE
from Christian Fellowship Publishers

By Watchman Nee

Aids to "Revelation"
Amazing Grace
Back to the Cross
A Balanced Christian Life
The Better Covenant
The Body of Christ: A Reality
The Character of God's Workman
Christ the Sum of All Spiritual Things
The Church and the Work – 3 Vols.
The Church in the Eternal Purpose of God
"Come, Lord Jesus"
The Communion of the Holy Spirit
The Finest of the Wheat – Vol. 1
The Finest of the Wheat – Vol. 2
From Faith to Faith
From Glory to Glory
Full of Grace and Truth – Vol. 1
Full of Grace and Truth – Vol. 2
Gleanings in the Fields of Boaz
The Glory of His Life
God's Plan and the Overcomers
God's Work
Gospel Dialogue
Grace Abounding
Grace for Grace
Heart to Heart Talks
Interpreting Matthew
Journeying towards the Spiritual
The King and the Kingdom of Heaven
The Latent Power of the Soul

Let Us Pray
The Life That Wins
The Lord My Portion
The Messenger of the Cross
The Ministry of God's Word
My Spiritual Journey
The Mystery of Creation
Powerful According to God
Practical Issues of This Life
The Prayer Ministry of the Church
The Release of the Spirit
Revive Thy Work
The Salvation of the Soul
The Secret of Christian Living
Serve in Spirit
The Spirit of Judgment
The Spirit of the Gospel
The Spirit of Wisdom and Revelation
Spiritual Authority
Spiritual Discernment
Spiritual Exercise
Spiritual Knowledge
The Spiritual Man
Spiritual Reality or Obsession
Take Heed
The Testimony of God
The Universal Priesthood of Believers
Whom Shall I Send?
The Word of the Cross
Worship God
Ye Search the Scriptures

The Basic Lesson Series
Vol. 1 - A Living Sacrifice
Vol. 2 - The Good Confession
Vol. 3 - Assembling Together
Vol. 4 - Not I, But Christ
Vol. 5 - Do All to the Glory of God
Vol. 6 - Love One Another

ORDER FROM: 11515 Allecingie Parkway Richmond, VA 23235
www.c-f-p.com

ORDER FROM: 11515 Allecingie Parkway Richmond, VA 23235
www.c-f-p.com

www.ingramcontent.com/pod-product-compliance
Lightning Source LLC
La Vergne TN
LVHW051551080426
835510LV00020B/2950